Enslaved Women in America

The African American History Series

Series Editors:
Jacqueline M. Moore, Austin College
Nina Mjagkij, Ball State University

Traditionally, history books tend to fall into two categories: books academics write for each other, and books written for popular audiences. Historians often claim that many of the popular authors do not have the proper training to interpret and evaluate the historical evidence. Yet, popular audiences complain that most historical monographs are inaccessible because they are too narrow in scope or lack an engaging style. This series, which will take both chronological and thematic approaches to topics and individuals crucial to an understanding of the African American experience, is an attempt to address that problem. The books in this series, written in lively prose by established scholars, are aimed primarily at nonspecialists. They focus on topics in African American history that have broad significance and place them in their historical context. While presenting sophisticated interpretations based on primary sources and the latest scholarship, the authors tell their stories in a succinct manner, avoiding jargon and obscure language. They include selected documents that allow readers to judge the evidence for themselves and to evaluate the authors' conclusions. Bridging the gap between popular and academic history, these books bring the African American story to life.

VOLUMES PUBLISHED

Booker T. Washington, W.E.B. Du Bois, and the Struggle for Racial Uplift
Jacqueline M. Moore (2003)

Slavery in Colonial America, 1619–1776
Betty Wood (2005)

African Americans in the Jazz Age: A Decade of Struggle and Promise
Mark Robert Schneider (2006)

A.Philip Randolph: A Life in the Vanguard
Andrew E. Kersten (2006)

The African American Experience in Vietnam: Brothers in Arms
James Westheider (2007)

Bayard Rustin: American Dreamer
Jerald Podair (2008)

African Americans Confront Lynching: Strategies of Resistance from the Civil War to the Civil Rights Era
Christopher Waldrep (2009)

Lift Every Voice: The History of African American Music
Burton W. Peretti (2008)

To Ask for an Equal Chance: African Americans in the Great Depression
Cheryl Lynn Greenberg (2009)

The African American Experience During World War II
Neil A. Wynn (2010)

Through the Storm, Through the Night: A History of African American Christianity
Paul Harvey (2011)

Enjoy the Same Liberty: Black Americans in the Revolutionary Era
Edward Countryman (2011)

A Working People: A History of African American Workers Since Emancipation
Steven A. Reich (2013)

Between Slavery and Freedom: Free People of Color in America from Settlement to the Civil War
Julie Winch (2014)

Enslaved Women in America: From Colonial Times to Emancipation
Emily West (2014)

Enslaved Women in America

From Colonial Times to Emancipation

Emily West

ROWMAN & LITTLEFIELD
Lanham • Boulder • New York • London

Published by Rowman & Littlefield
A wholly owned subsidiary of The Rowman & Littlefield Publishing Group, Inc.
4501 Forbes Boulevard, Suite 200, Lanham, Maryland 20706
www.rowman.com

Unit A, Whitacre Mews, 26-34 Stannary Street, London SE11 4AB, London

British Library Cataloguing in Publication Information Available

Library of Congress Cataloging-in-Publication Data Available

978-1-4422-0871-1 (cloth : alk paper)
978-1-4422-0873-5 (electronic)

∞™ The paper used in this publication meets the minimum requirements of
American National Standard for Information Sciences—Permanence of Paper
for Printed Library Materials, ANSI/NISO Z39.48-1992.

Printed in the United States of America

Contents

~

Chronology

1619: The first African slaves arrive in Virginia.

1641: Massachusetts recognizes slavery in its legal codes through The Body of Liberties.

1643: Virginia lawmakers levy a tax (tithe) upon the labor of African slave women. Amended to include free black women in 1668.

1656: Elizabeth Key sues for and gains her freedom in Virginia.

1662: Virginia law decrees that enslaved children should follow the status of their mother.

1667: Virginia defines "negro" people as "separate" from Christians, closing off baptism and formalized Christianity as a possible route to freedom.

1676: Bacon's Rebellion in Virginia.

1691: Virginia forbids interracial marriage and all interracial sexual acts.

1708 and 1712: Slave riots in New York City.

1724: Louisiana's Code Noir forbids the "barbarous and inhumane" treatment of the enslaved.

1739: Stono Rebellion in South Carolina.

1753: Phillis Wheatley born in Boston.

1770: Pennsylvania legislates for the gradual emancipation of slaves.

1773: Phillis Wheatley becomes the first enslaved person to publish a book of poems.

1775: The thirteen colonies begin armed conflict with the British.

1775: Dunmore Proclamation offers freedom to slaves who support the Crown.

1776: Members of the Continental Congress sign the Declaration of Independence.

1776: Jenny Slew uses the courts to gain her freedom in Massachusetts.

1779: Clinton Proclamation offers enslaved women, as well as men, the chance to serve the British.

1779: New York State legislates for the gradual emancipation of slaves.

1781: Elizabeth, or "Mum Bett," gains her freedom in Massachusetts on the grounds that the state constitution of 1780 declared "all men are born free and equal."

1783: Treaty of Paris recognizes American sovereignty.

1789: Adoption of the U.S. Constitution.

1789: George Washington signs the Northwest Ordinance into law.

1791: Revolt begins in French Saint-Domingue.

1793: Eli Whitney patents the cotton gin.

1800: Gabriel Prosser attempts to lead a slave rebellion in Virginia.

1803: The Louisiana Purchase opens up new markets for the westward slave trade.

1804: Haiti declares independence.

1804: New Jersey legislates for the gradual emancipation of slaves.

1808: The international trade in slaves is outlawed.

1819: Slaves freed by their owners in Virginia have to leave the state.

1819: Acquisition of Florida from Spain.

1831: Mary Prince publishes her autobiography, *The History of Mary Prince, a West Indian Slave*.

1843: Isabella Baumfree changes her name to Sojourner Truth and begins campaigning for women's rights and emancipation.

1845: J. Marion Sims begins medical experimentation on enslaved women.

1848: William and Ellen Craft escape slavery in Georgia.

1849: Harriet Tubman escapes slavery and becomes involved in the Underground Railroad.

1850: Fugitive Slave Act.

1855: Celia murders her master, Robert Newsom, and is later hanged in Fulton, Missouri.

1860: William and Ellen Craft publish *Running a Thousand Miles for Freedom*.

1861: Outbreak of the Civil War.

1861: Union forces gain control of South Carolina's Port Royal Sound.

1861: Harriet Jacobs publishes *Incidents in the Life of a Slave Girl*.

1863: Lincoln's Emancipation Proclamation frees slaves in areas of rebellion.

1863: Confederate Impressment Law.

1864: U.S. War Department issued an order permitting all general hospitals under U.S. jurisdiction to hire African American women as cooks or nurses.

1865: Confederate defeat ends the Civil War.

1865: Thirteenth Amendment abolishes slavery in the United States.

1866: Former slave, Mattie Jackson, publishes her autobiography, *The Story of Mattie J. Jackson.*

1868: Fourteenth Amendment grants African Americans civil rights.

1877: Compromise of 1877 ends Reconstruction.

1891: Former slave Lucy A. Delany publishes her autobiography, *From the Darkness Cometh the Light, or, Struggles for Freedom.*

1898: Former slave Kate Drumgoold publishes her autobiography, *A Slave Girl's Story.*

1902: Former slave Susie King Taylor publishes *Reminiscences of My Life in Camp: An African American Woman's Civil War Memoir.*

1909: Former slave Annie Burton publishes her autobiography, *Memories of Childhood's Slavery Days.*

1930s: Works Progress Administration holds interviews conducted with thousands of elderly ex-slaves in the Southern states.

Introduction

Enslaved women's exploitation as black females took many different forms across time and space in North America. But from the moment traders first captured African women until bondage's dying days at the end of the Civil War, all enslaved women suffered, and all were exploited—to varying degrees—as both workers and reproducers. Some of the punishment white men and women doled out caused physical pain and suffering, while other forms of oppression resulted in personal anguish and heartbreak when owners wrenched families apart in the pursuit of profit. Most sinister of all was the sexual abuse white men inflicted upon enslaved women. Assaulters regarded black female bodies as ripe for brutal exploitation that resulted in owners' acquisition of yet more valuable infant slaves for free. Some women did not survive the onslaughts of bondage, but others fought, resisted, and survived through the refuge and support they gained from other slaves, be they mothers, sisters, children, husbands, or other female friends. Female bondage in America left a legacy of strength under adversity as enslaved women fought against their dual exploitation as mothers who reproduced and women who worked.

Throughout the course of American slavery, masters struggled to decide whether their enslaved women were primarily workers or reproducers as they continuously exploited their female chattel as both. Indeed, enslaved women's unique position sometimes led to horrific forms of treatment as masters sought both to punish people and to protect their property's value. On the Hess plantation in Tennessee, the owners abused their pregnant female slaves by making them dig holes in the ground to shelter their unborn

1

children while they whipped them. Marie Hervey, one of their slaves, had dreadful memories of this unique punishment. But it also illustrated slaveholders' ultimate dilemma. Anxious to punish their female slaves to assert their authority and ownership, masters nonetheless also recognized that the women carried valuable future chattel inside them. Moreover, because white slaveholders never decided whether slave women's labor or their children were most important to them, they continued to exploit enslaved women as both workers and as mothers, continuing female slaves' dual exploitation for the duration of bondage.

Chapter 1 of this book traces the evolution of female slavery in America from its origins in West Africa. It sketches the lives of precolonial African women before comparing the lives of enslaved women in America with female slaves elsewhere in the Americas, including Brazil and the Caribbean. Chapter 2 traces the development of female enslavement during the colonial period of American history, when laws defining slave status through the female line rendered enslaved women as profit-making reproducers of valuable slave babies. Slavery existed throughout North America, but, as the third chapter shows, the institution became a uniquely Southern phenomenon in the aftermath of the revolution, largely due to the invention of the cotton gin and the subsequent commercialization of Southern agriculture.

Following the revolution, especially after the abolition of the international slave trade in 1808, the enslaved population of the United States moved from being primarily African to American born, and slaves created new cultural forms that were less "African" and more "American" in scope. Female slaves developed new ways in which they attempted to survive and protest their status as chattel, the possessions of their masters. Enslaved women regarded the revolutionary conflict practically, and through the chaos and upheaval of war they sought to preserve their families and avoid the potentially devastating impact of war on their everyday lives.

The fourth chapter focuses on the lives of enslaved women in the Southern states in antebellum times: from the 1808 closing of the international slave trade until the outbreak of the Civil War in 1861. The chapter explores women's relationships with their owners, their work patterns, and white people's abuse of their female chattel. Moreover, it examines how women in bondage carved out their everyday lives despite white exploitation and the constant threat that their owners might separate them from their loved ones by selling them away. It also traces important roles women played within their families and their communities as well as the various ways in which they resisted their enslavement. The Civil War era forms the backbone of chapter 5. The horrendous conflict that wrenched the United States in two and

ended the institution of slavery, provided enslaved women with new challenges and opportunities for geographic mobility. Left alone on plantations
and farms with their white mistresses, female slaves also realized they were
no longer bound to white women, and relationships between the two quickly
deteriorated. The epilogue considers life for freedwomen after the Thirteenth
Amendment abolished slavery in 1865. Liberty brought great joy, but white
Southern racism continued, and white hostility and oppression made it hard
for freedwomen to live and work according to their own values during the
Reconstruction era. A selection of primary source documents allows readers to
explore for themselves the experience of enslaved women, and a bibliographic
essay outlines some of the major published works on the topic.

Historical writings about enslaved women have evolved and changed
over time. The exclusion of women from traditional historical analyses was
fairly common until the influence of social history and a "second wave" of
feminism during the 1960s and 1970s encouraged historians to redress past
imbalances. Historians of the 1950s, including Kenneth Stampp and Stanley Elkins, had assumed that enslaved families took "matriarchal" forms in
which women dominated "emasculated" men who were unable to protect
and provide for their women and children. They also assumed female slaves
performed no housework, cooking, making clothes, or nursing. But evidence
from enslaved women themselves shows how, at home, female slaves did indeed cook, nurse, clean, and make their clothes, all in addition to performing
strenuous and exhausting labor for their white masters. Stampp and Elkins'
arguments reflect an idealized notion of 1950s domesticity, which holds that
men should protect and provide while women's roles center on the domestic
realm. Historians are products of their time, and this is as true for historians
of American slavery as it is for anyone else.

Later generations of "revisionist" historians rejected the view of enslaved
families as "matriarchal" (dominated by women). Seeking to overturn the
controversial Moynihan Report of 1965, which placed the "blame" for
problematic, dependent, single-parent African American families upon the
"legacy" of bondage, historians of this era, most of whom were men, stressed
that enslaved families were instead patriarchal in nature, with strong men
acting as heads of households. Thus, enslaved women were, yet again,
perceived only in relation to their roles within immediate families and not
on their own terms. Activist Angela Davis, however, inspired by her own
involvement in Black Power protest and the women's movement, pioneered
the notion of "triple exploitation" of enslaved women as blacks, slaves, and
women. A growing body of scholarship about the lives of *white* Southern
women since the 1970s also influenced a boom in the number of books and

articles about enslaved women. These works highlighted the complexity and diversity of enslaved women's lives and moved beyond overly simplistic "matriarchy versus patriarchy" arguments.

This generation of historians grappled with enslaved women's everyday lives, including their work patterns and their personal relationships. Deborah Gray White promoted the ways in which white masters and mistresses stereotyped enslaved women as "Jezebels" or "Mammies," and these images of females in bondage explain a great deal about white rationalizations of slavery. Although they did not exist in reality, both Jezebel and Mammy convey how white people *thought* enslaved women behaved. Jezebel and Mammy were polar opposites: Jezebel tended to be young, while Mammy was more mature. Jezebel was lithe and attractive, whereas Mammy was fearsome and stout. Typically light skinned, Jezebel served to legitimize in the eyes of white men their sexual exploitation of enslaved women because Jezebel herself was innately promiscuous. Indeed, her alleged rampant "African" sexuality was out of control. An innately racist image, Jezebel thus enabled white men to claim their female slaves both initiated and desired intimate sexual liaisons, even though white men forced themselves upon enslaved women against their will. The Jezebel stereotype also allowed white women to place the blame for interracial sexual liaisons solely at the feet of enslaved women rather than on their own husbands, fathers, or sons.

Mammy, Jezebel's polar opposite, idealized and glorified the domestic labor of female slaves, especially prominent, middle-aged cooks who ran plantation households. White women and men often remembered Mammy affectionately following the end of the Civil War. Many white Southerners wrote personal reminiscences of slavery with a sense of wistfulness. But in reality Mammy was as much a fictitious stereotype as Jezebel. White masters and mistresses convinced themselves that Mammy, their most trusted house servant, of whom they were terribly proud, was happy, contented, and devoted to her white "family," even though this was not true. In reality, enslaved women who achieved positions of power, status, and prestige within their owners' "Big Houses" used the benefits of their position to assist other enslaved people, and they prioritized their relationships with enslaved communities over and above those they had with white men and women. For example, house servants illicitly passed on food and other supplies as well as news to other slaves. Mammies listened to white conversations in the kitchen, the parlor, and at the dinner table, and they discreetly passed on information about forthcoming events to other enslaved women. Sometimes news was good—their owners might be organizing a corn shucking, party, or Christmas dance, or increasing rations in the slave quarters. However, at other times news from the "Big House" was less positive as owners talked to each other about punishing or selling "troublesome" slaves. Thus, rather than being "loyal and devoted" to her "white family," Mammy was often the eyes and ears of the slave quarters in the Big House.

There has been a lot of scholarship on female slaves since the pioneering work of historians during the 1970s and 1980s. Historians have shown how enslaved women, be they domestics or field laborers; residing on plantations, on farms, or in cities; living in colonial, revolutionary, or antebellum times, lived through their oppression in a variety of different ways and in different contexts. Enslaved women's health and reproduction over the course of their life cycle has also attracted significant historical inquiry, and historians now commonly investigate enslaved women's lives via their relationships with each other, with enslaved men, with their children and other family members, wider kin and community networks of enslaved and free people of color, their white masters and mistresses, and other members of white communities. Yet despite all their interactions with others, at the same time all women in bondage certainly shared characteristics only with each other; namely, their dual exploitation as workers and as reproducers.

Historians' growing recognition of the wide range of available primary sources for studying female slavery has contributed to the proliferation of writings about enslaved women. Such primary evidence includes the published autobiographies of enslaved women; more "traditional" source materials left by white slaveholders about their female slaves, for example their letters, diaries, and plantation record books; and over two thousand Works Progress Administration (WPA) interviews with former slaves conducted in the Southern states during the 1930s. The WPA narratives provide unique testimony about the everyday lives of ordinary enslaved women, although from a researcher's perspective they raise a number of concerns. The majority of female WPA interviewees were less than ten years old in 1865, so their memories of bondage are those of enslaved children. The respondents' memories could also have dimmed with age because most were over eighty years old at the time they were interviewed. Moreover, most interviewers were white, and during the time of the Depression and racial segregation, some female interviewees were no doubt extremely reticent to divulge details of private or distressing experiences during slavery to younger whites, especially if the interviewers were men. Some of the elderly African American respondents hoped that their interviewers would help them obtain old-age pensions, resulting perhaps in a desire to please. Moreover, the fact that African Americans experienced high poverty rates during the Depression of the

1930s may have led many respondents to regard their childhoods in slavery more positively than their experiences of old age.

But these methodological concerns notwithstanding, other than a few published female slave narratives, there is simply no other primary source on which historians can draw to explore details of the everyday lives of enslaved women from their own perspective. Moreover, the methodological concerns about WPA evidence can be countered. Some of the experiences of bondage recounted by women interviewed by the WPA mirror those depicted in the few autobiographies published by enslaved and formerly enslaved women. Furthermore, even though the majority of respondents were children during bondage, they described not just their own lives but also those of other family members, including mothers and fathers, aunts and uncles, grandparents, and others in their enslaved communities. Although elderly when interviewed, female respondents also remembered a great deal about slavery. Also, while understandably reticent to share with white interviewers intimate details on private and taboo subjects such as white men's sexual assaults, not all formerly enslaved women felt this way. Some of the women were extremely frank and recounted incidents of sexual violence and brutality during bondage. Their evidence also suggests that not all respondents viewed slavery through an overly positive prism, as some scholars have claimed. Although the testimony of formerly enslaved women is not always completely candid, it provides historians with unique insights into the female slave experience. Used in conjunction with a range of other primary sources both from and about enslaved women, WPA evidence allows historians of female slavery to construct a more complete picture of enslaved women's lives.

A small number of women published autobiographies that recounted their personal experiences of bondage. However, such written testimony is rare since Southern laws forbade whites to teach slaves to read or write, and only a tiny minority of female slaves was literate. Nonetheless, some exceptional women did publish their autobiographies and reminiscences, including Harriet Jacobs, Annie L. Burton, and Mattie J. Jackson. Their narratives mostly focus on their dramatic escape from bondage and their subsequent involvement in the fight for abolition in the Northern states. Indeed, most female autobiographers hoped to evoke the sympathy of abolitionist campaigners. Thus, just like WPA testimony, some historians have questioned the validity of these autobiographies, claiming that they constitute mere abolitionist propaganda written by white ghostwriters who exaggerated the brutality, degradation, and violence of slavery in the hope of gaining support for their cause. However, extensive and meticulous research by historians, including Jean Fagan Yellin, shows that Harriet Jacobs's depiction of bondage was indeed accurate, and that slavery was just as brutal as Jacobs described it. Like WPA testimony, these autobiographies provide a unique window into slavery from the perspective of enslaved women.

Historians have also sought to reconstruct female slaves' lives through "traditional" source materials, such as the letters, diaries, plantation record books, advertisements, bills of sale, wills, legal petitions, and other surviving testimony from their masters and mistresses. Female slaves appear frequently in masters' plantation record books and journals, especially when they were sick or bore a child. Some owners also recorded the marriages and family groupings of their slaves, for example, in their bills of sale that tended to list slaves within their own family units that were then parceled together in larger lots. From white owners' bills of sale, historians can commonly see marriage patterns and single-parent families, enslaved women's ages, and the number and ages of children in their family groupings.

Plantation mistresses and other white women also referenced enslaved women in their letters and diaries. For example, Mary Boykin Chesnut and Frances Anne Kemble describe at length their relationships with female slaves, and they convey some of the complexities of gendered relationships that crossed the racial divide. White men also occasionally made reference to their enslaved women in their more personal letters and journals. For example, James Henry Hammond described in his diary his sexual relationship with one of his female slaves. So although white sources do not reveal the perspectives of enslaved women, they provide a framework from which historians can draw broader conclusions about the lives of female slaves.

Historical research has revealed many aspects of the everyday lives of enslaved women, but putting this picture together has not been easy. Mostly illiterate and exhausted from providing for their owners, themselves, and their families, female slaves have, sadly, left relatively few written testimonies that historians can peruse. Thus, scholars have to rely upon multiple primary sources and fragments of evidence to build up a picture of the main contours of enslaved women's lives. And historians can also speculate. They can try to imagine themselves in the position of a female slave and her available choices at a particular point in time. Indeed, historian Stephanie Camp argued that when surviving testimony is scant (as in the case of many enslaved women), then historians must rely upon their own imagination and speculation to ascribe meanings to remaining documents. This point is vital for any historian seeking to understand, and to empathize, with the enslavement of women in America in all its ramifications.

CHAPTER ONE

~

Enslaving African Women

Before bondage took hold in the Americas, various forms of slavery existed in precolonial West Africa. The transatlantic slave trade and the horrors of the Middle Passage changed the institution for good, but family formations and female work patterns among American slaves and members of precolonial West African societies often bore surprising similarities to each other. Both African heritage and white Euro-American cultural influences played roles in the lives of enslaved women, although sometimes maintaining their African traditions proved difficult. Across the broad geographical context of the Americas, enslaved women's lives all displayed significant similarities as well as important differences in terms of the everyday challenges women faced. For example, enslaved women in South America and the British and French Caribbean toiled stoically under harsh conditions on vast sugar plantations where imbalanced sex ratios meant there were more men than women. Conversely, in North America, with its more equal sex ratios, many more enslaved women lived in family units with their husbands and children than did female slaves in South America and the Caribbean. Slaveholders across the Americas preferred to purchase and use the labor of captured male Africans, but only in North America did enslaved people have a natural increase, where births exceeded deaths, and enslaved women were obviously crucial to this process. Women enabled North American slavery's unique development as they stood at the heart of slaves' exploitation as laborers and as reproducers.

Approximately twelve million Africans began the Atlantic crossing to the Americas, but around only 10.5 million survived the terrible journey known as the "Middle Passage." This transatlantic movement of people was literally the midpoint of the triangular trade that crisscrossed the Atlantic Ocean. In the first stage, traders from Europe carried goods such as sugar, tobacco, iron, gunpowder, and cloth to Africa's West Coast, which they then bartered in exchange for African people. They sold captured Africans who survived the Middle Passage as slaves in the new worlds of America and the Caribbean islands. Finally, the traders brought the produce of the New World—primarily sugar and tobacco—to sell in Europe before returning again to West Africa with more goods for sale and barter. Typically, males made up more than half of all slave shipments across the Atlantic, with adult men in the majority. The proportion of adult men shipped also rose over time, as did the number of children. The transatlantic slave trade gained its chattel from a huge geographic area of around 3,500 miles along the West African coast and about 5,000 miles inland, but the main areas from which captives left Africa's West Coast varied over time. In the fifteenth century the majority of slaves came from Senegambia, but by the early sixteenth century the West Central African regions assumed dominance of the trade that lasted until its ending. Increased British trade from 1670 onward saw the Bight of Benin and the Gold Coast emerge as significant slave-exporting areas, while by the eighteenth century the Bight of Biafra and Sierra Leone became dominant exporters of African slaves, as the map on page 11 shows.

Significantly, between 1619 and 1808 (when the international trade in slaves legally ended), only around four hundred thousand Africans came to the shores of North America in total because the great majority of newly enslaved people (between 90 to 95 percent) went to South America and the Caribbean, where the demand for enslaved labor was higher. The map (p. 12) shows where the majority of captive Africans disembarked in the New World between 1501 and 1867, because some countries continued to import slaves after the 1807 international ban and some even landed in the United States after this date due to the continuation of a small, illegal, international trade there. Geographic origins influenced where slaves might arrive in the New World. Some 60 percent of those who left from the Bight of Benin disembarked in Bahia, Brazil, while a similar percentage of slaves who arrived in the Caribbean originated in the Bight of Biafra or the Gold Coast. The Bight of Biafra also exported more female slaves to the New World than any other region of the African coast.

Slavery had always existed in various forms within West Africa, although the institution was more flexible and malleable than the transatlantic slavery that superseded it. African enslavement did not necessarily mean bondage for life, and many women enslaved in West Africa lived both as slaves and

Map from David Eltis and David Richardson, *Atlas of the Transatlantic Slave Trade* (New Haven and London: Yale University Press, 2010), 15.

free people at different points over the course of their lives. West Africans used many words to convey the different kinds of bondage existing in their societies. For example, some men held enslaved women in marriage contracts or as concubines, but more commonly societies acquired whole groups of slaves of both sexes through warfare, who they might subsequently free at a later date. Because West African slavery was less rigid than the enormous transatlantic slave trade based upon the long-distance sale of black people, the arrival of European traders on Africa's West Coast permanently altered not just African slavery, but the whole of West African society, forever. A transatlantic trade based on external demand outside Africa began to replace West Africa's preexisting slave systems, and racial difference became the

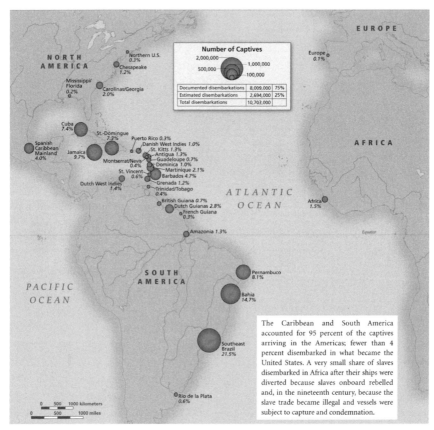

The Caribbean and South America accounted for 95 percent of the captives arriving in the Americas; fewer than 4 percent disembarked in what became the United States. A very small share of slaves disembarked in Africa after their ships were diverted because slaves onboard rebelled and, in the nineteenth century, because the slave trade became illegal and vessels were subject to capture and condemnation.

Map from David Eltis and David Richardson, *Atlas of the Transatlantic Slave Trade* (New Haven and London: Yale University Press, 2010), 17.

paramount distinguishing feature of this new trade in slaves. Africans found themselves increasingly at risk of being kidnapped, sold to European traders in exchange for goods or weapons, and shipped across the Atlantic Ocean from where they would never return.

Researching the lives of women in West Africa both prior to and during the transatlantic slave trade has proven immensely difficult for historians because surviving written testimony is scant. Nevertheless, by supplementing their research with that conducted by anthropologists, historians have been able to sketch a broad picture of women's lives in precolonial West Africa, from where most American slaves came. Divided by traders into three geographic zones of Upper Guinea, Lower Guinea, and the Congo/Angola, there was considerable diversity in the life experiences of women in these areas, although all West African women tended to partake in agricultural production, either at subsistence level or by making exports crucial to regional economies. For some women, this meant the adjustment to agricultural labor in the Americas was not as great as it might otherwise have been because women were familiar with hard, physical outdoor work, just not forced labor under the threat of a whip.

Because of West Africa's vast size, women's lives were diverse, although as daughters, wives, mothers, and grandmothers all West African women shared certain characteristics over the course of their lives. Familiar with agricultural production and hard, outdoor labor, the majority of West African women played active roles in their local and regional economies. Women raised crops and livestock, and in some areas, such as the Western Gold Coast, they sold and bartered food and textiles at large, biweekly markets. Some women traveled great distances to trade. For example, Mandinka women from the Upper Guinea coast used waterways of rivers and swamps to transport goods and food from one area to another for sale or barter, and traveling on these waterways also enabled socialization. West African women's active economic roles subsequently allowed traders and slaveholders conveniently to perceive these women as innately "suited" to a life of manual labor outside in the hot fields, in contrast to white indentured servants. So the great majority of enslaved women labored outside, although their work patterns developed in different ways across the Americas.

West African family formations also varied across time and space. European traders often drew a contrast between their own norms and customs and what they perceived to be matriarchal West African societies where women ruled. But male and female partners often ruled together as a pair—for example, among the Fon people—while other women, including members of the Yoruba, lived within clans or extended family networks. Many West African societies, including the Fon, Ewe, and Igbo tribes, traced their descent though men in patrilineal fashion, but others, for example, the Fante people, lived within matrilineal societies in which people traced their descent through a female line. Thus, West African women had many different experiences. Within clan-based societies, elders (mostly men) organized and legitimized women's marriages. Wedlock involved an exchange of goods and services, although for many societies, blood relationships assumed priority over conjugal ties, rendering births and deaths more significant than marriage itself. Wealthy men practiced polygamy (multiple marriage) much more than the poor, because only rich men could afford to keep several wives, some of whom were bound to wealthy men through enforced contracts.

West African marriage patterns displayed more similarities with patterns of wedlock in preindustrial Europe than with marriage among antebellum slaves or in modern-day societies. Enslaved people in America, devoid of possessions and property, were early pioneers in marrying for modern notions of romantic love, whereas in precolonial West Africa (and premodern Europe), most women entered wedlock for economic factors and to bind extended families or clans together. Singing, dancing, and feasting constituted important elements of traditional African courtship rituals, just as they were among American slaves. For example, Umbanda women sang songs welcoming new brides to their village, and Mende and Temne people practiced circular dances that later became known as the "ring shout" in North America. Conjurers and sacred charms also played an important role in courtship practices on both sides of the Atlantic.

After marriage, men and women of West African societies operated together to regulate fertility. Long periods of sexual abstinence after giving birth were commonplace, and because breast-feeding often lasted for up to three years, West African mothers participating in agricultural labor strapped their children to their backs and carried them most of the time. Traditional African childcare practices made the jolt of enslavement even harder to bear. Enslaved women tried hard to maintain their patterns of fertility regulation in the New World, but callous masters pressured them into frequent childbearing, and they also suggested the early weaning of infants to reduce dependence on mothers. Prescribed infant food such as ground rice was often of low nutritional value and sometimes even harmful to young and delicate digestive systems. Masters also perceived the practice of women taking their babies with them to the fields as detrimental to hard labor, so slaveholders instead encouraged their chattel to leave their infants with other enslaved women. Unable to maintain their practical and beneficial African reproductive and child-rearing traditions when enslaved in the Americas, enslaved women faced a new dual exploitation as workers and as reproducers.

The growth of the transatlantic slave trade drastically altered the economic roles and family lives of those remaining in West Africa, where some patterns had remained in place for centuries because more men left than women. In some areas these newly imbalanced sex ratios resulted in population decrease, but this was not always the case. In Angola, for example, women outnumbered men by two to one by the end of the international trade in 1808. But a well-established system of polygamy meant women continued to reproduce well, although the reduction in adult males of working age inevitably made women's workload heavier as well as more varied. In West African societies where men hunted and fished, their capture and sale across the Atlantic left women deficient in protein, which affected fertility levels. The transatlantic slave trade disrupted local markets and economies, and it also left behind many older and younger dependents in West Africa, people unwanted by the traders as slaves. These young children and grandparents needed women to care for them, women who had sometimes been sold away. So unnatural population profiles rose, and life became very difficult. The slave trade had immense consequences on both sides of the Atlantic world.

Slave traders commonly separated captured men and women in West Africa's coastal ports, seeing sexual difference as a logical and easy way to categorize their prisoners. Thus began a process of gender separation that continued throughout American slavery across the New World. The percentage of African men that traders shipped across the Atlantic also rose over time because women's value within regional local trades decreased the willingness of local slavers to make them available to the Atlantic trade. Moreover, traders themselves considered slaves primarily in terms of their role as workers, not reproducers, so they paid more for men than women, and they considered men aged between fifteen and thirty as the most valuable. Negotiating sales in coastal ports, traders held men and women separately in crowded pens or occasionally underground dungeons, sometimes for a matter of weeks, at other times for several months in dark, dank, and unsanitary conditions. Before departure, traders stripped men and women for intrusive physical examinations, a process particularly shameful for women because traders attempted to assess women's potential to reproduce as well as their value as laborers. Unbeknownst to women, this invasive experience would be repeated again on the other side of the Atlantic Ocean when they arrived in the New World. In Africa some traders branded their human cargo on their backs, chests, shoulders, or thighs. Usually, branding was to avoid any confusion over ownership, but sometimes traders branded people in case they needed to claim compensation if a new slave died. The practice of branding survived into the New World, but it mostly died out by the nineteenth century as abolitionist pressure rose.

When ships were ready for departure, traders took their captured Africans— be they Fante, Bakongo, Yoruba, Ewe, Akan, Melimba, Angola, Igbo, or from another tribe—from their holdings, and forced them onto dark and crowded wooden ships in what must have been a terrifying ordeal. Although exact sex rations remain unknown, men made up the majority of people (there were two to three men to every one woman) on the life-altering, horrific Middle Passage across the Atlantic that could take about three months. Around one-fifth to one-quarter of the human cargo were children, and as with the adults, males predominated because of traders' belief in the superior laboring abilities of boys and men. Famous images, such as that of the *Brookes* slave ship below, tend to depict only men in the ship's hold and omit women altogether, despite the presence of a number of women and girls onboard the large, crowded ships.

Sailors onboard slave ships separated women and children from men because they believed captured men to be more likely to protest and revolt

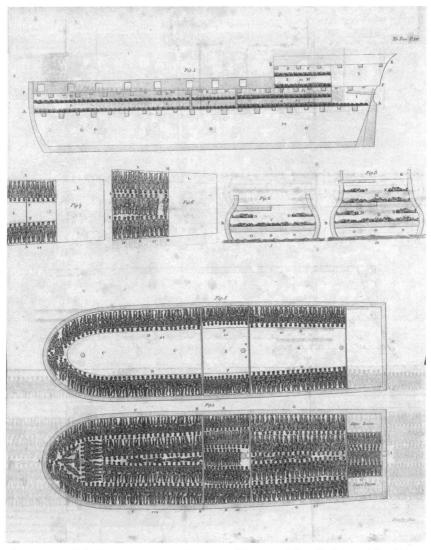

The History of the Rise, Progress, and Accomplishment of the Abolition of the African Slave-Trade by the British Parliament. HT1162. C6 1808 v.1. Special Collections, University of Virginia, Charlottesville, Virginia.

than women. So sailors forced men into chains at the very bottom of ships where they could barely move in the darkness and stench. Because sailors considered women less "risky" cargo, they often allowed them onto the upper decks, or the quarterdeck, and sometimes they left them unchained for the duration of their enforced Atlantic journey. However, despite women's marginally preferable material treatment, the conditions for all human cargo remained cramped and unsanitary, enabling disease and sickness to rampage through the ships' stale air. Men and women both suffered from flux, apoplexy, malaria, smallpox, and yaws. But women suffered the added risks of losing children through miscarriages or stillbirths, and sometimes women themselves lost their lives due to pregnancy, childbirth, or postnatal illness. Other women became sick because they could not adequately tend to their monthly menstrual cycles in a hygienic manner.

In his autobiography, former slave Olaudah Equiano remembered children falling into foul tubs where people emptied their bladders and bowels, women shrieking, and the dying groaning. Food and water remained scarce because sailors prioritized their own needs above those of their human chattel, and sailors sometimes simply hurled dead bodies overboard. Sometimes captured African men and women took their lives into their own hands and flung themselves into the sea if they were able to. Alexander Falconbridge, a former slave ship's surgeon, described in 1788 how one "dejected" woman refused both food and medicine, telling an interpreter she only wanted "to die" before passing away on the ship. Women who came onto the upper decks enjoyed the chance to see clearly and breathe in fresh, salty air. But unbeknownst to them, some sailors only brought black women onto the decks so they could fulfill their own sexual desires. Well aware that captured men remained chained up on the bottom decks, unable to help their women, sailors brutally and intimately assaulted their female cargo. Women who resisted these sexual assaults displayed immense personal bravery in fighting off crewmembers. For example, in 1792 a British slave ship captain was tried for the death of a fifteen-year-old girl who had apparently refused to "dance naked" for him. Other women resisted their new oppression by inducing abortions, jumping overboard, attempting suicide, and by engaging in physical fights with sailors. More women than men poisoned their crew's food, because sailors frequently kept women near storerooms on the upper decks. Inevitably, sailors impregnated some women, so from the beginning of bondage to its end, sexual abuse both characterized and differentiated women's slavery from that of men.

Upon arrival on the other side of the Atlantic, traders sold the majority of African people in Brazil and the Caribbean islands, and only around 5 to 10 percent of all African imports ended up in British North America following their terrifying transatlantic journey. Of these, the percentage of women decreased from 41.1 percent for the years between 1663 and 1700 to 36.0 percent between 1701 and 1800 as traders increasingly brought men from Africa. Newly enslaved women brought with them to the New World a useful ability to labor and to reproduce, the latter proving to be of vital significance in North America, where an excess of births over deaths resulted in a growing slave population. As a whole, diversity characterized enslaved women's lives across the Americas and the Caribbean because slavery developed in different ways depending on geographic context, crops grown, methods of production, and patterns of ownership and labor.

In the early days of the transatlantic trade, most slaves disembarked in Brazil, as the Portuguese gradually transferred their slave-based sugar plantations from Atlantic islands such as Madeira across the Atlantic to northeastern Brazil. A sugar economy also developed in the Caribbean islands, fueled by an ever-growing European sweet tooth, and by the 1660s Barbados had a thriving sugar economy cultivated by Africans. Jamaica followed suit after the British took the island from Spain in 1665, and France likewise developed a prominent sugar economy across the Caribbean. The rise of sugar fostered the growth of slavery. Because sugar was so very difficult to cultivate, Caribbean masters preferred enslaved men to women as the former were physically strong enough to cut the heavy sugarcane. In the long term, this high demand for enslaved men, for slaves as workers rather than reproducers, led to imbalanced sex ratios throughout Caribbean slave societies. Hard labor, inadequate nutrition, and relatively few women compared to men resulted, unsurprisingly, in a natural decrease in the enslaved population as the number of deaths exceeded births.

Sugar masters still condemned enslaved women to hard labor in the sugarcane fields even as they regarded women's work as inferior to men's. Masters also preferred men for more skilled roles such as drivers or carpenters, although by the 1670s a few very wealthy planters made a connection between enslaved women and domestic servitude and used some women as house slaves. But most women labored in the sugarcane fields, their roles as workers superseding women's reproductive abilities in the eyes of those who held them in bondage. In the early 1700s, for example, 322 men and 216 women lived on one Jamaican plantation. But while female slaves made up the majority of field laborers, half of the enslaved men performed skilled roles, including drivers, stock workers or keepers, and craftsmen. The harsh Caribbean regime also adversely affected enslaved women's fertility. Planters displayed little interest in their slaves' familial relationships or their female chattel's reproductive capacities because (unlike North American planters) they regarded their female slaves primarily as laborers. For the duration of slavery, life was incredibly difficult for enslaved women in the Caribbean islands, as testimony from Mary Prince's 1831 autobiography conveys. Mary cultivated salt in the hot sun and slept in a dormitory at night. Throughout the Caribbean, brutal overseers compelled enslaved women into strenuous work with difficult crops, while their owners, in contrast, lived lives of opulence and luxury far away in their European homes.

The lives of women enslaved in the colonies and countries of South America had more parallels with those of slave women in the Caribbean than with North America's female slave population. As was the case in the Caribbean islands, sugar drove the economic development of Brazil, first as a Portuguese colony and then after independence, although crops such as coffee became increasingly important over time. As in the Caribbean, Brazilian slavery was characterized by its preponderance of enslaved men because owners preferred male labor. But a system of urban enslavement also developed in Brazil, where women labored in their masters' homes. There were also relatively large numbers of free people of color because the Catholic Church fostered manumissions, and masters commonly freed their female slaves. Some enslaved women in the Caribbean and Brazil lived in volatile worlds because attempted slave revolts, largely male led, were more common than in North America, as were maroon communities of runaway slaves, known as *quilombos* in Brazil. Brazilian slaves, such as those in the Caribbean, experienced natural decrease as more slaves died than were born, again in contrast to North American enslavement. Gang labor systems for the cultivation and production of sugar were simply not conducive to long and healthy lives among slaves, male or female, and so Brazilian and Caribbean slaves had shorter life spans than their North American counterparts. A natural decrease of slaves in Brazil continued despite the continuation of large, illegal trade in slaves there from Africa that ended only in 1850.

Over time, Brazil's sugar industry steadily declined, and by the midnineteenth century most sugar came from Cuba where the crop was grown cheaply and more efficiently. Moreover, a thriving domestic trade in slaves within Brazil's vast terrain destroyed family networks and enslaved communities just like the domestic slave trade within the nineteenth-century United States. Overall, Brazil's enslaved women experienced very diverse forms of slavery. Women on northern sugar plantations lived different lives from those enslaved further south, where the production of leather and jerked beef grew in the early nineteenth century as sugar became more unprofitable. Likewise, women on the vast coffee estates of the interior had different life experiences again, while urban slave women in major cities such as Rio de Janeiro mostly worked as domestics within their owners' homes. But like North American slaves, Brazilian enslaved women entered stable and long-lasting monogamous marriages when they were able to, and Brazilian masters also freed more enslaved women than did North American slaveholders. The Catholic Church sometimes fostered manumissions, but the relative shortage of white women was an important factor here because many Brazilian slaveholders entered intimate relationships with their enslaved women and then subsequently freed their partners, and sometimes their children, too. Brazil was also the last country of the Americas to abolish slavery in 1888, although women were at the heart of a more gradual process of abolition here and in Cuba, where "free womb" measures introduced in the early 1870s created opportunities for women to make legal claims for freedom on the basis of their motherhood.

In the Caribbean, the harshness of the slave regime led to frequent outbreaks of sickness, disease, and rebellion among enslaved people, and European abolitionist pressure about the brutality of bondage also rose over time. Britain and France abolished slavery in their colonies in 1834 and 1848, respectively, whereas slavery in the United States only ended with the Southern defeat in the Civil War in 1865. Haiti was the only country in the Americas to end enslavement by means of a successful revolt, which began in French Saint Domingue in 1791 and ended with Haiti declaring independence in 1804. Although the country was sadly plagued by domestic turmoil thereafter, the Haitian revolt indirectly affected enslaved women in North America because it reduced the number of manumissions as owners became ever more anxious about the existence of free people of color whom owners believed might entice their slaves into similar rebellion.

African women arriving on the shores of British North America, such as those elsewhere in the New World, had no idea about what their future might hold. Like the traders in African coastal ports on the other side of the Atlantic Ocean, men interested in buying female slaves poked, prodded, and subjected women to invasive physical examinations in their attempts to gauge both the potential labor and reproductive capacities of their likely new chattel. Slaveholders bought women from auction blocks in major coastal ports such as Charleston, where trading ships docked. Thereafter, women destined for plantation labor underwent a process known as "seasoning," designed by masters to break people's spirits and obliterate African cultural identities. Yet the newly enslaved African women of the New World resisted such attempts through developing their own "Creole" culture in which slaves shared and molded their diverse African backgrounds and traditional practices into new cultural forms.

Not all African women were destined for the developing system of Southern plantation slavery. America had thirteen colonies, all of which had some enslaved women living within their borders, and slavery developed much differently in the Northern states from those further south. Diversity characterized the lives of enslaved women in colonial times, but throughout North America, where only 5 to 10 percent of captured Africans disembarked, a unique set of circumstances fostered the development of an ever-growing slave population. Whereas there were only 698,000 slaves in North America in 1790, by 1860, just before the Civil War, slave owners held four million people in bondage in the southern United States. This increase, of course, would not have been possible without enslaved women reproducing more and more new slaves. This phenomenon of natural increase differentiated North American slavery from systems of bondage elsewhere, and in North America slaveholders increasingly regarded their female bondswomen as both laborers and reproducers at the same time. Enslaved women stood at the very core of this emerging and unique regime.

CHAPTER TWO

~

Enslaved Women in
the Colonial Era

Slavery existed in all of the thirteen colonies that would become the United States (see Table 2.1). Surviving evidence only reveals the number of black people in America, and not their sex or how many were enslaved. But slave women formed an important part of the American colonies, a continent rich in natural resources and ripe for exploration and exploitation. Though they did not realize it themselves when they first arrived, enslaved women would increasingly be at the heart of the violence and brutality that characterized America's slave economy. After all, it was the exploitation of female slaves as workers and as women that enabled colonial America to grow and prosper.

Until the late seventeenth century, poor, white, European migrants to America frequently worked as indentured servants, and the number of black slaves in America was relatively small. Colonists also employed and enslaved Native Americans. So it was by no means clear that the American economy would become so dependent upon black slave labor. For example, estimates suggest that in 1625 there were only twenty-three people of African descent in Virginia. By 1650 that number had grown to around three hundred, compared to a total Virginia population of 18,700. Moreover, not all black people were slaves—some men and women were either born free or obtained their freedom through manumission. Indeed, the first group of Africans who arrived in Virginia in 1619 was indentured servants. But slowly, the number of white indentured servants declined, as landowners increasingly realized that enslaved

Table 2.1.   Numbers of Slaves, by Colony, 1680–1770 (Estimates of blacks as a percentage of the population in brackets)

Colony	1680	1700	1720	1750	1770
North					
New Hampshire	75	130	170	550	654
	(3.7)	(2.6)	(1.8)	(2.0)	(1.0)
Massachusetts	170	800	2,150	4,075	4,754
	(0.4)	(1.5)	(2.4)	(2.2)	(1.8)
Rhode Island	175	300	543	3,347	3,761
	(5.8)	(5.1)	(4.6)	(10.1)	(6.5)
Connecticut	50	450	1,093	3,010	5,698
	(0.3)	(1.7)	(1.9)	(2.7)	(3.1)
New York	1,200	2,256	5,740	11,014	19,062
	(12.2)	(11.8)	(15.5)	(14.3)	(11.7)
New Jersey	200	840	2,385	5,354	8,220
	(5.9)	(6.0)	(7.7)	(7.5)	(7.0)
Pennsylvania	25	430	2,000	2,822	5,561
	(3.7)	(2.4)	(6.5)	(2.4)	(2.4)
South					
Delaware	55	135	700	1,496	1,836
	(5.5)	(5.5)	(13.2)	(5.2)	(5.2)
Maryland	1,611	227	12,499	43,450	63,818
	(9.0)	(10.9)	(18.9)	(30.8)	(31.5)
Virginia	3,000	16,390	26,550	107,100	187,600
	(6.9)	(28.0)	(30.3)	(43.9)	(42.0)
North Carolina	210	1,000	3,000	19,800	69,600
	(3.9)	(3.9)	(14.1)	(25.7)	(35.3)
South Carolina	200	3,000	11,828	39,900	92,178
	(16.7)	(42.8)	(70.4)	(60.9)	(60.5)
Georgia	n/a	n/a	n/a	600	15,000
	(n/a)	(n/a)	(n/a)	(19.2)	(45.2)
Totals					
North	1,895	5,206	14,081	30,172	47,710
	(2.3)	(3.6)	(5.2)	(4.8)	(4.4)
South	5,076	23,752	54,577	212,346	430,032
	(5.7)	(21.1)	(27.7)	(38.0)	(39.7)
Thirteen Colonies	6,971	28,958	68,658	242,518	477,742
	(4.6)	(11.1)	(14.8)	(20.2)	(21.4)

Table taken from Peter Kolchin, *American Slavery* (London: Penguin, 1993), 240, and Ira Berlin, *Generations of Captivity: A History of African-American Slaves* (Cambridge, MA and London: Belknap Press, 2003), table 1.

labor was cheaper and hence more efficient in a climate of emerging global markets. The international trade in African slaves, raw materials, and consumer goods therefore increased over time. The triangular trade between the New World colonies, Europe, and Africa generated unrivaled profits for white colonists who grew ever more dependent on obtaining maximum labor—and consequently maximum wealth for themselves—from a race-based system of agricultural slavery.

Diversity characterized the lives of enslaved women in colonial America because bondage itself was based on distinct agricultural economic systems. These systems all used enslaved labor, but Northern colonies remained societies with slaves rather than slave societies, in contrast to the South, where society became increasingly organized around the slave system at the heart of its economic production and societal values. In the Northern colonies, without plantations, most enslaved women lived on small family farms with their white owners. However, in the Southern colonies, cash crops led to a growing demand for plantation labor. In the seventeenth century, the Chesapeake area imported the largest number of slaves to plant and harvest tobacco. In the eighteenth century, South Carolina and Georgia colonists, planting rice and indigo, took the lead. South Carolina had begun to import slaves from Barbados in the mid-seventeenth century, and by 1708 it became the only mainland colony with a black majority, its rapidly developing rice culture causing a boom in the number of slaves imported to the area.

Throughout the American colonies, women arriving as slaves found themselves part of a growing institution that gathered further strength as preconceived notions about innate black or African "inferiority" gained momentum among white people. White Americans increasingly deemed black Africans, male or female, to be inferior, suitable only for hard, manual labor within houses or fields, and they moved away from using white indentured servants as their slave ownership grew. Nonetheless, despite their preconceived notions of black racial inferiority, whites valued enslaved labor and sought ways to increase the number of slaves they owned, creating a long-term dilemma about whether enslaved women's status derived primarily from their status as workers or reproducers.

White colonial Americans developed laws that sought to define the legal status of slaves, including women and their children. In the Northern colonies, the Puritan founders of Massachusetts used the Old Testament to support slavery in their society. Drawn up in 1641, the Puritans' Body of Liberties outlined ways in which a person might legitimately be enslaved through warfare, being sold into bondage, and selling oneself into slavery. The Body of Liberties also outlined how slaves should be treated. Chattel enjoyed certain rights such as owning property, and they could sue or be sued in courts. But the evolution of racism in the colonies also subjected enslaved women to new restrictive laws, especially in the Southern colonies where slavery was developing as a large-scale, profitable agricultural enterprise. Beginning in 1643, Virginia lawmakers levied a tax (tithe) upon the labor of African slave women. Masters of female slaves had to pay the tithe for their slaves, thus making enslaved women dependents of white owners rather than of their spouses. But the colony imposed no similar tax on white women's labor. These legal distinctions between black and white women grew more pronounced over time. After 1668, the tax also applied to free black women, which placed them under an immense burden, as they had to pay it themselves. These laws convey the growing significance of race to colonial policymakers, who increasingly perceived white women primarily as dependents rather than workers. In contrast, policymakers, and, over time, broader society, viewed free black and enslaved women first and foremost as workers, and slave women merely as full dependents of their white masters.

Before policymakers formulated laws regulating slaves, the offspring of enslaved women often faced an uncertain legal status in the colonies. In 1656 in Northumberland County, Virginia, Elizabeth Key, the daughter of an enslaved woman, petitioned for her freedom on two grounds. In her first claim she argued that, as a Christian woman, she should not be subjected to enslavement. Key put forward her second claim against enslavement on the grounds that she was the daughter of a free, white English man. Elizabeth Key's petition displays a keen awareness of the association of enslavement with "heathen" Africans. While legislators initially declared her free, they later deemed her a slave after an appeal by the administrators of her master's estate. Elizabeth Key was certainly resilient—she finally obtained her much-longed-for freedom after marrying her white lawyer. Tellingly, her status was thus still dependent on her relationship to a man. Overall, this case illustrates colonial lawmakers' dilemmas about how to define legally enslaved and free black women and their offspring, as well as the role of wedlock in defining women's status.

In 1667, Virginia defined "negro" people as "separate" from Christians, closing off baptism and Christian conversion as a possible route to freedom for slaves. But enslaved women across the Northern and Southern colonies continued to protest their status. For example, in 1776 Jenny Slew used the courts to gain her freedom in Massachusetts, where enslaved people could still bring civil suits in court. Born to a white mother and black father, Slew had been kidnapped and enslaved by a white man named John Whipple before becoming the first enslaved person ever to win her freedom by jury trial.

Facing a growing number of freedom suits in a climate of evolving white ideas about the significance of skin color to systems of slavery, Virginia, and subsequently other colonies, moved toward the legal separation of men and women of different races. Beginning in 1662 in Virginia, in a practice later replicated elsewhere, enslaved children followed the legal status of their mothers as slaves. This act was unusual for its time because most laws tended to render women dependent on their relationship to men. The law also strengthened the assumption of most whites that slavery was "natural" for black people. More importantly for slave women, the 1662 law gave slave-hungry masters every incentive to sexually assault their enslaved women who might then bear them valuable children. Moreover, Virginian law deemed the paternity of slave children meaningless in its attempt to diminish enslaved fathers' influence over their enslaved offspring. These new slave laws stood in contrast to legal customs affecting white society, and they permanently affected enslaved women's lives. Slaveholders now increasingly began to regard their female slaves as both laborers *and* potential reproducers for white men's future economic enterprises.

At the same time, colonial lawmakers moved toward the criminalization of interracial sexual relations, but they failed to enforce the law in relation to white men and black women, probably because so many white men subjected black women to sexual assault. Bacon's Rebellion of 1676, led by Nathaniel Bacon and a group of fellow frontier landowners against Governor William Berkeley, also further provoked white fears about the number of free black people in Virginia and their interactions with whites. Concerned with the lack of support from the governor against Indian attacks on the frontier, Bacon's supporters offered freedom to indentured servants and slaves who fought with them in the rebellion. The idea of white indentured servants fighting with black slaves terrified many wealthy Virginian lawmakers who felt the need to promote racial separation. Following the rebellion, a number of white women faced prosecution for committing sexual offenses with black men. However, it was not until 1691 that Virginia forbade interracial marriage and all interracial sexual acts. Law enforcement increasingly targeted white women for bearing mixed-race children while white men went unpunished. Indeed, white men's sexual relations with their enslaved women conveniently increased slaveholders' supply of chattel and potential profits, giving them every incentive to abuse and harass their female slaves.

Slaves began to trickle into French Louisiana in the early decades of the eighteenth century, and in 1724, the colony's application of the Code Noir formalized enslavement there. For example, a batch of regulations forbade any "barbarous and inhumane" treatment of the enslaved. But Louisiana did not always enforce these laws, and some masters subjected their enslaved women to appalling physical punishment and sexual abuse. With its mixture of French, Spanish, and Catholic traditions, slavery developed somewhat differently in Louisiana. Masters manumitted slaves more often than in the Anglo societies further north and east, and free people of color constituted a larger percentage of the overall population in Louisiana when compared to elsewhere in North America. There were also more interracial marriages. Indeed, entering into wedlock with white men was of particular significance to enslaved women because it provided an opportunity for them to escape bondage via manumission, as white men often freed their enslaved partners. But while some of these relationships offered enslaved women a path to freedom and some economic security, they could also be perilous. The Code Noir denied slaves the protections of legal marriage, and many enslaved women waited in vain for freedom that never arrived, or witnessed their white husbands free their children while they themselves remained forever in bondage.

By the eighteenth century, as the number of people held in bondage grew ever larger, Virginia and the other Southern colonies had enacted a whole series of codes and laws designed to prohibit interracial marriage and formalize legal enslavement. The South's economy grew increasingly dependent on slavery, in contrast to the Northern colonies, where slavery was less legally defined and less significant to economic development. Virginia's laws provided important benchmarks for the status and treatment of slave women that other colonies later replicated. Race and enslavement became increasingly associated with ideas about innate inferiority that had particular implications for enslaved women. Because female slaves were black, white colonists perceived them as an important new source of agricultural labor in the emerging plantation economies of the South.

Owners valued their female slaves as laborers *and* as mothers, but at times those two roles came into conflict with each other. While colonial slave owners valued slave women primarily as laborers, they were also well aware that only as mothers could their female chattel reproduce their labor force. In order to do so, they needed respite from the demands of slave labor. Female slaves learned they could sometimes use their childbearing ability as a way to negotiate an improved quality of life from their masters and mistresses. Slaveholders grappled with this dilemma throughout slavery; however, in the colonial era they primarily exploited their female slaves as workers since they could easily import additional slaves from West Africa. Slave owners often questioned how much time off slave women needed to bear and rear children when caring for offspring also meant losing a day of manual labor. Enslaved mothers had to bring their babies with them to the fields strapped to their backs while they worked, a practice women carried over from Africa. In short, slaveholders did not spare slave women the rigors of field labor because of their gender as they increasingly spared upper-class white women from outdoor work.

White men expected enslaved women to produce more than white women because they perceived them to be physically stronger than their white counterparts. Yet at the same time, masters considered their slave women's work as worth only three-quarters of that of enslaved men, while they commonly regarded children as a "half share" by the age of nine or ten.

Masters gave enslaved women the most tedious and monotonous forms of fieldwork, including preparing ground, digging ditches, hoeing, and weeding. They also expected women to clean and tidy communal areas such as stables, and to spread manure as a fertilizer. Their sex made slave women's work lives both boring and difficult. Moreover, because West African women often had some prior agricultural experience, including tobacco and rice cultivation, they performed their labor well, which facilitated further exploitation of their labor as plantation economies began to boom. In the minds of white slaveholders, black women were capable of hard physical labor and were consequently a source of rising profits. Some slaveholders took pride in the ability of their slave women to labor as hard as men. In the long run, white people came to see field labor as inappropriate for white people and suitable only for "inferior" black men and women.

The development of a plantation-based economy facilitated by black female labor in the South opened up opportunities for male slaves to develop valuable skills and trades, including working as blacksmiths, carpenters, tanners, and shoemakers. While slave owners trained some of their male slaves in this skilled work, they typically denied these opportunities to women, confining them to the drudgery of unskilled field labor, plus undertaking some spinning and weaving cloth to make into clothes at the end of the day. Nonetheless, a minority of slave women had some opportunities to develop skills. Lowcountry women wove baskets or made quilts drawing on skills they learned in Africa, while others worked in plantation dairies or raised poultry. Some women became midwives or "root doctors," again sometimes using skills and knowledge they acquired in Africa. But all too often, white owners forced their female slaves to use their skills *in addition* to other labor they expected of them. Masters and mistresses expected their female slaves to weave, sew, or quilt at night *and* to work in the fields or the plantation house during the day, whereas owners permitted enslaved men to labor at their skilled trade *instead* of performing fieldwork. These divisions grew more pronounced in the antebellum era with the consolidation of the plantation regime.

Within the Southern colonies, different types of labor systems emerged in the Virginia and Maryland Chesapeake and South Carolina and Georgia lowcountry areas. Enslaved women in the Chesapeake worked under a "gang" labor system from sunup to sundown, in which a group of slaves worked together. But in the lowcountry coastal areas of South Carolina and Georgia, a "task" system of labor evolved, in which slaves had to complete a designated amount of work, after which their time was their own. Some enslaved women growing rice under the task system benefitted from their prior experience of rice cultivation in Africa because it granted them a small amount of free time. Having specific tasks to perform and living within large slave communities allowed enslaved women and men to develop a relatively autonomous black culture that was characterized by a degree of independence. The task system of labor therefore offered considerable benefits to enslaved women, who were free to labor at their own pace. If they worked extremely hard, they could take advantage of the "reward" of free time at the end of the working day to complete their own household chores or to spend valuable time with their loved ones.

But laboring under the task system was not easy for enslaved women. Under the task system, rice became the staple crop of the swampy and humid South Carolina lowcountry by the eighteenth century. Both men and women labored in the rice fields, in hot, sticky, wet, and arduous conditions. The inhospitable climate negatively affected enslaved women's health, despite commonly held white beliefs that African slaves were "better suited" to laboring in the rice swamps. Rice had a fourteen-month growing season. Early in the year, slaves cleared all land of shrubs and bushes. Women then planted seed in the spring and thereafter weeded and hoed crops throughout the hot summer months. Enslaved women worked in unhealthy water that sometimes reached as high as their knees, if not their waists. Later in the year, slaves harvested, stacked, threshed, pounded, and milled rice crops to remove the precious kernels from their husks. Initially, enslaved women used mortars and heavy pestles to mill rice, which could weigh up to ten pounds. It was not until the 1760s that mechanized threshing began to replace these centuries-old techniques.

Although the task system offered a degree of freedom during the working day, it was not always advantageous for enslaved women. For example, new mothers took longer to complete their allotted tasks because they constantly had to break away from their work to feed their infants. New mothers and pregnant or elderly women sometimes suffered from exhaustion that slowed their pace of work. But the task system did provide enslaved women with some spare time that allowed them to tend to their own gardens or patches of land where they grew vegetables or raised a few animals. Planting vegetable gardens improved women's quality of life as it supplemented inadequate diets and provided opportunities to sell or barter goods, all of which continued into the antebellum era.

The gang system that emerged on the wheat and tobacco plantations of the Chesapeake area led to greater separation of men and women in comparison to the lowcountry. Under the supervision of a black driver or white overseer, enslaved women often performed different work than men and were commonly separated from "sundown to sunup" for at least five days of the week. For example, slave men harvested wheat with a scythe, while masters relegated women to the roles of gatherers and stackers. Likewise, carting and plowing tended to be the preserve of men, but women put up fences, cleared out stables, and leveled ditches. This sexual division of labor substantially altered the everyday working lives of slave people. While working only with other women could provide support and camaraderie for female slaves, it also left them more vulnerable to sexual assault from masters or overseers.

Regardless of the type of system under which they labored, all fertile enslaved women endured frequent pregnancies in the name of their masters' profits, some of which were the result of their owner's, or other white men's, sexual assaults. Significantly, the colonies passed no laws to limit the amount of work slave women could partake in during pregnancy or after giving birth, and white owners simply made their own decisions about how much they should exploit their enslaved women as workers and as mothers. Practice therefore varied according to individual preferences. For example, in 1759, Chesapeake planter Richard Cobin instructed his overseers: "The Breeding Wenches more particularly you must be kind and Indulgent to, and not force them when with child upon any Service or hardship that will be Injurious to them."[1] Cobin prioritized the reproductive abilities of his slave women, but not all others followed his example, especially in colonial times. Other slave women in the South faced the almost impossible endurance test of trying to bear and raise their children while also performing hard agricultural field labor under the task or gang system.

As the slave population of America rose, slaveholders began to perceive the women they held in bondage differently. They viewed female slaves less as workers who were inferior to male slaves and more as prime reproducers of a valuable and unique labor force. Indeed, white masters increasingly fostered racist notions that black women were innately suited to childbearing and rearing and were naturally promiscuous. In 1756, Reverend Peter Fountain, of Charles City County, Virginia, proclaimed that black females were "far more prolific than . . . white women," and Reverend Francis Le Jau wrote in 1709 that "one of the most Scandalous and common crimes of our Slaves is their perpetual Changing of Wives and Husbands."[2] Of course, such ideas justified further the exploitation of female slaves as reproducers as well as laborers.

Unsurprisingly, combining labor and motherhood in this way had a detrimental impact on slave women's mental and physical health. Rates of stillbirth, infant mortality, and early childhood mortality among the enslaved stood at more than 50 percent in colonial times. The natural decrease of the enslaved population in the early years of settlement only slowly gave way to natural increase within established colonies, although the pattern was not universal. Because slave women had inadequate diets lacking in protein and owners subjected them to the hard rigors of agricultural labor or housework, enslaved women's fertility was lower than it might otherwise have been, despite the lack of contraception and the attempts of their owners to force or otherwise cajole slave women into having frequent offspring.

Nonetheless, Virginia's slave population, due to a combination of natural increase and the continued importation of enslaved people across the Atlantic, began to grow ever more rapidly from the second decade of the eighteenth century. Slave women bore more children than was necessary to replace the preceding generation. The South Carolinian slave population also began to experience natural increase in the second half of the eighteenth century. Black and white women's fertility rates rose over the colonial period, from forty-two births per one thousand in 1670 to fifty-eight per one thousand in 1789. But enslaved children's lives remained precarious, and many infants fell prey to early mortality. Enslaved women also bore their first children at a relatively young age, typically in their late teens, and their children were born close together, mostly between twenty-five and thirty months apart. The majority of enslaved women therefore gave birth about every other year and bore many children over their lifetime, not all of whom survived.

Even as their female slaves bore many children, colonial slaveholders exploited enslaved women primarily for their labor under task or gang systems. But the profits generated by enslaved women led to the development of large, luxurious plantations in the Southern colonies of South Carolina and Virginia. So some owners moved some of their female slaves out of the fields and into their own grand mansions, known as the "Big House." Enslaved women within those homes were particularly at risk of sexual assault and physical violence by whites because they often lived and worked within the Big House. Colonial mistresses could be particularly cruel to their slave women, especially when they suspected their husbands of engaging in illicit sexual liaisons with their female slaves. In 1748 Hannah Crump, of Lancaster County, Virginia, was accused of murdering a slave woman named Jenny, who belonged to her husband. Hannah might have suspected that the two were intimately involved, and Jenny bore the brunt of her wrath regardless of whether her relationship with Hannah's husband was forced or consensual. William Byrd recorded in 1711 the quarrels of his wife and her female slave, Jenny, after which he "soundly whipped" Jenny. By the 1730s Byrd also recorded his extramarital sexual liaisons with his female domestics. Despite being in his late sixties, Byrd described the events in his secret diary as "playing the fool."[3] Owning enslaved women whom he kept in his house thus allowed William Byrd to affirm his sexual prowess despite his advanced age. His actions, like those of other elite white men, illustrate the power of white men in colonial American society, and the mental and physical violence directed against enslaved women within white people's houses grew more pronounced over time.

As enslaved women moved out of the fields and into their owners' Big Houses, they became more vulnerable to sexual abuse by white occupants. Surviving evidence about the sexual abuse of female slaves at the hands of white men is very scant for this early period of American history. But many sexual assaults undoubtedly occurred in the colonial era, especially following the Virginia law of 1662, which decreed slave children follow the status of their mothers, because the law effectively exempted white men from paternity liability. Significantly, there are no surviving records of rape convictions against white men, whether they were the victim's owner or not, for assaulting enslaved women between 1700 and the Civil War, indicating that whites did not see the sexual assault of black women as a crime.

Nonetheless, there is evidence of interracial sexual relationships. An undated painting from the colonial era depicts a white man enjoying both his interracial liaison with a black woman and his physical punishment of a black man, both "Virginian luxuries" (see p. 34).

In 1775, a Virginia Baptist church board heard accusations that one of its members had practiced "the act of uncleanness to a Mulatto girl of his own."[4] In 1773, a court in Delaware brought a bastardy charge against a white man for impregnating his slave. Similarly, one year later, Philip Vickers Fithian noted repeated sexual attempts on Sukey, a "likely" slave girl of sixteen, by the son of her master, Robert Carter III. Many more unrecorded incidents of sexual relations between white men and their female slaves occurred, because enslaved women often bore mixed-race children. Effectively trapped, with no protection from the law, these women's only support came from their own networks of family and friends. Sometimes enslaved men attempted to protect their womenfolk from white men's abuse. In the 1790s, Josiah Henson's father attacked an overseer who tried to rape his wife, Henson's mother. But this brave and gallant attempt to protect his wife had dire consequences. Henson's father's overseer severed his slave's ear and subjected him to one hundred lashes. Henson's father's white owner then sold him from his home in Maryland to Alabama.

Because of the profits it generated, enslaved women's fertility was of great concern to their white masters, who often at the same time held scant regard for the sanctity of these women's marriages. Indeed, slaveholders sometimes parceled out slaves in their wills, hoping to maximize the chances of enslaved

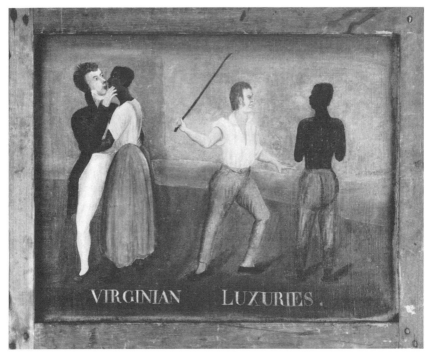

Image of *Virginian Luxuries*, undated and unsigned. Courtesy of the Abby Aldrich Rockefeller Folk Art Center, The Colonial Williamsburg Foundation, Virginia. Museum Purchase.

offspring being born to their descendents, for example, by pairing slaves of the opposite sex in their bequests. Slaveholders also replaced dead, sold, or escaped slaves with men and women whom they hoped would bear children together in the hope of maximizing reproduction. One observer noted with some surprise that the Spanish governor of Florida rejected an enslaved woman offered to him. "The Governor does not understand plantation affairs so well as some of us Southern folks," he wrote. "Nancy is a breeding woman and in ten years time may have doubled her worth in her own children."[5]

Masters implicitly recognized female slaves' humanity by allowing slave marriages, even though the law did not sanction them. Yet at the same time they displayed great inhumanity toward their enslaved women by selling and separating married slave couples and their children in the pursuit of profit. Such tensions remained largely unresolved through the antebellum era, characterizing a continuity of oppression of female slaves as workers and as mothers who generated for white men profits from both their labor and their reproduction. Masters frequently separated their female slaves from their enslaved spouses in the pursuit of profit. Marriage had existed in many different forms in precolonial West Africa, from where traders brought most slaves to the colonies and most enslaved people continued to enter wedlock of some form. At wedding ceremonies they might exchange gifts, following traditional African customs. Some African forms of polygamy survived across the Atlantic, although the practice never became widespread in America and was more common among lowcountry slaves who lived in large groups and continued their African cultural traditions. Some owners' estate lists identified enslaved families in which husbands had more than one wife and children were born to different wives, but such instances appear to have been fairly uncommon. Enslaved women mostly entered into wedlock as the sole wives of their husbands, with whom they formed long, loving, and monogamous relationships. Slaves in the American colonies also underwent a process of "creolization" as they bore children on American soil. They ceased to be African and became enslaved Americans instead.

But even as slaves became more "Americanized," white society still deemed the marriages of enslaved men and women not worthy of legal recognition because the law considered slaves themselves as not human beings in their own right, but merely chattel or possessions. Early South Carolina legislation of 1715 had made reference to enslaved "husbands" and "wives." But policymakers began to shy away from promoting legal marriage for enslaved people in their drive to emphasize the significance and desirability of racial separation. The legal status of their wedlock placed another irony at the heart of enslaved women's lives because the promotion of marriage could have been an opportune route for masters seeking to increase their supply of slaves. However, some masters saw monogamous marriage as a barrier to maximizing slave women's reproductive potential. For example, one North Carolina writer observed in 1737 that masters should encourage their enslaved women to take a "second, third, fourth, fifth and more Husbands or Bedfellows" if there were no children after a "year or two."[6] Ironically, such behavior only furthered stereotypes about the alleged moral inferiority and promiscuity of blacks.

The South Carolina Stono Rebellion of 1739 also affected masters' attitudes toward enslaved reproduction. Led by African-born slaves, the revolt generated fear within white society about the continued importation of slaves from Africa who might be prone to rebellion. Rather than importing slaves from Africa, white slaveholders began to regard the encouragement of female slaves' fertility as an easier way to increase the colonies' supply of slaves. For at least a decade after the rebellion, policymakers raised the duties on imported slaves so high that the importation of enslaved men and women from Africa and the Caribbean to the Carolinas essentially ceased.

Childbirth was thus the easiest way for owners to maintain, if not increase, their stock of chattel.

Encouraging frequent pregnancies put masters on the road to conflict with their enslaved women, who resented their owners' interference in all matters related to their choice of spouse and the number of children they bore. Enslaved women also grew ever more exhausted as they combined frequent childbearing with hard physical labor. Displaying feelings of bitterness and resentment toward their callous and interfering owners, colonial enslaved women resisted their oppression in various ways, including trying to limit the number of children they bore and sometimes by escaping their bondage altogether. Although colonial enslaved women undoubtedly loved their children and the men they married, they had to be pragmatic. Evidence suggests female slaves brought knowledge of plants that could induce miscarriages with them from Africa, which some women used to restrict the number of children born of white men's sexual abuse. Others aborted any pregnancies simply because they did not want to raise their children as chattel. Running away from hated owners was easier for colonial enslaved women than those who lived in later years of slavery, because over time white society grew more adept at tracking and capturing runaway slaves, especially following the Revolution. But in colonial times, there existed small groups of maroon (runaway) slaves in the swamplands of the Carolinas and elsewhere in the colonies, and Spanish Florida was a haven for enslaved refugees. The first recorded group of slaves escaped from Carolina to Florida in 1687, and included two women, an infant girl, and eight men. They escaped by boat to St. Augustine, where the two women worked as domestics for the Spanish governor. All the escapees subsequently converted to Catholicism. So began a pattern of slave flight south where the fugitives hoped the Spanish authorities would free them.

That enslaved women who were mothers escaped bondage in colonial times defies the notion that all female slaves with children were bound to their owners through their offspring. But overall more men than women escaped bondage. Runaway figures from the *South Carolina Gazette* from 1732 to 1737 show that of the 195 advertisements for runaway slaves, males outnumbered females by three to one. Men were more likely to flee together, while women mostly ran away alone, a testament to the bravery of enslaved women. Colonial runaway slave advertisements also note couples escaping together, suggesting that their marriages were just as important to them as their freedom.

The daily experiences of slave women often depended on the size of the plantation on which they worked. Enslaved women who lived on large Southern plantations—holdings consisting of around twenty slaves or more—had opportunities to gain support from other enslaved women, whether they labored in the Big House or in the field. Women's camaraderie and friendships helped them to survive the trials of their enslavement. But women held in bondage on small farms did not have the same support networks. On the outer reaches of the Carolina frontier, slave women lived in isolation and poverty, eking out a day-to-day existence with their owners and tending cattle or other animals. On the late eighteenth-century Tennessee frontier, white families tended to buy enslaved women singly, meaning they would live separately from family and friends, leading to further heartbreak, loneliness, and isolation. The everyday lives of these "nonplantation" slave women reflected the routines of enslaved women in the Northern colonies and those working as Southern domestic servants. These women typically lived in close proximity with the white families who owned them, often isolated from broader community networks of support and without a sympathetic person with whom they could share their feelings of exhaustion and exasperation.

Bondwomen belonging to white families who possessed only a handful of enslaved people had to be adept at a broad range of tasks while laboring for their owners. Dividing up the work of their enslaved people into the broad categories of "house" and "field" made no sense on smallholdings, and enslaved women had to perform all kinds of labor depending on the ever-changing needs of their owners. Frequently, too, blacks and whites worked alongside each other during harvest season. Living with white owners in these more intimate environments sometimes led to closer and more personal relationships across racial lines. However, such intimacy often resulted in enslaved women's physical or sexual abuse at the hands of whites. Moreover, because they were poorer than planters, small-scale slaveholders gave their chattel less food, more scanty clothes, and inferior housing when compared to those enslaved on plantations. Geographical location thus significantly affected enslaved women's life experiences.

The majority of Northern enslaved women lived in relatively small households with their white owners and perhaps their own immediate family members. Yet the North always remained a society with slaves rather than a slave society, in contrast to the South. Around fifteen thousand black women lived in the Northern colonies on the eve of the Revolution, the majority of whom were enslaved, but some were free. Free black women had either been born free, manumitted by their owners, had purchased themselves, or had been bought by a family member. Overall, the dividing line between slavery and freedom was more flexible and malleable in the North than on Southern plantations. As a result, more Northern black women moved out of bondage and into freedom. The Northern economy was also more diversified than the Southern plantation-centered economy. In the Northern colonies, enslaved women grew a variety of crops including wheat, while others worked in the dairy and cattle industries or raised other livestock. Some masters employed their female slaves in modern factory settings such as mills, while other enslaved women worked as domestics in their owners' homes.

Like their Southern counterparts, enslaved women in Northern colonies resisted bondage. For example, the main arsonists of the New York City slave riots of 1708 and 1712 were allegedly women. Northern enslaved women also attempted to run away. In 1758, a Westchester County slave named Bridget conspired with six others to run away but was caught and punished. Northern enslaved women also fought to maintain their families, to live in communities of their choosing, and to share their culture across generations. Some women excelled at storytelling or the arts. For example, Phillis Wheatley (1753–1784), born in Africa but raised as a slave in Boston, became a renowned poet as well as the first enslaved person to publish a book of poems. Other enslaved women partook in regional festivals and celebrations as African American culture evolved.

Throughout America's colonies, the lives of colonial slave women who lived in busy ports and cities, whether North or South, were quite similar. Slaveholders in America's emerging towns and cities needed female slaves, either those they owned or those they hired, to clean and maintain their urban homes and to cook and wash for white families. Whites brought enslaved women into urban environments with them, and these lively, bustling places brought new opportunities. Sometimes masters permitted their bondwomen to hire themselves out to make extra money—either for their white owners or for themselves—and women commonly found work as cleaners, washerwomen, cooks, and nannies, laboring as domestics rather than in the hot fields of the Southern plantations. Sometimes colonial enslaved women earned enough money to buy their freedom, or that of their family members, but others remained in bondage.

Colonial enslaved women had a visible presence in the public markets of Southern cities such as Charleston and Savannah, as well as other towns and cities where they sold products made either by them or by their family members. In Charleston, slave women used their quilting, basketmaking, and culinary skills, some of which had African origins, to sell fruit, vegetables, seagrass baskets, and other crafts in the city's markets. An observer in 1778 counted "sixty four Negro wenches selling cake, nuts, and so forth" in Charleston. However, racist regulation of public markets increased over time as white authorities grew more concerned about the "freedoms" they had afforded enslaved people in public places where slaves might socialize with other members of society. Lawmakers increasingly insisted that slaves hold permits or other forms of passes in order to sell their wares. In Savannah, a 1740 "Negro Act" permitted slaves to trade in city markets only on behalf of their owners, although some women violated the law by continuing to sell cheap foodstuffs on behalf of themselves so long as they had a pass from their masters. Slaves' market trading on Sundays also declined over time due to the growth of evangelical Christianity, which viewed Sunday trading as unchristian. Nonetheless, enslaved women living in or near cities had less monotonous, more independent, and increasingly mobile lives than those working on plantations in the South or family farms in the North.

While female slaves experienced better working conditions in cities and towns, they also faced stiff labor competition. Male slaves reaped the benefits of learning skilled trades such as carpentry or shoemaking. Skilled men also had the best chance of finding urban work, although in the Northern cities some enslaved women in the needle trades gained reputations as skilled spinners, knitters, weavers, and sewers. Free women of color, who were themselves often poor, were another source of competition. Nonetheless, urban slave women often cultivated friendships and other personal relationships with free people of color and at times even with poor whites. Unlike isolated plantations, towns and cities were hives of activity where enslaved women could go out and mix with a variety of people. Overall, slave women in urban environments lived in a wider world than did those on Southern plantations or Northern family farms, meeting new people, black and white, free and slave.

Over the course of the colonial period, whites enslaved black women within a variety of settings, rural and urban, coastal and inland, Northern and Southern, and on small family farms as well as large plantations. On the large Southern plantations, colonial slaveowners grew richer and richer from the profits generated by their exploitation of female slaves, primarily as workers, but ever increasingly as reproducers. Diversity characterized enslaved women's lives as they gradually changed from being African imports to becoming an African American enslaved labor force. But women's sex always affected their everyday work and community lives, and their everyday experiences were different from those of enslaved men.

Notes

1. Quoted in Lorena S. Walsh, *Motives of Honor, Pleasure and Profit: Plantation Management in the Colonial Chesapeake, 1607–1763* (Chapel Hill: University of North Carolina Press, 2010), 506.

2. Philip D. Morgan, *Slave Counterpoint: Black Culture in the Eighteenth-Century Chesapeake and Lowcountry* (Chapel Hill and London: University of North Carolina Press, 1998), 85. Reverend Francis Le Jau quoted in Sylvia R. Frey and Betty Wood, *Come Shouting to Zion: African American Protestantism in the American South and British Caribbean to 1830* (Chapel Hill and London: University of North Carolina Press, 1998), 49.

3. See Kathleen M. Brown, *Good Wives, Nasty Wenches, and Anxious Patriarchs: Gender, Race, and Power in Colonial Virginia* (Chapel Hill and London: University of North Carolina Press, 1996), 306, 332, 355–6.

4. Quoted in Sharon Block, *Rape and Sexual Power in Early America* (Chapel Hill and London: University of North Carolina Press, 2006), 65.

5. Quoted in Philip Morgan, *Slave Counterpoint*, 94.

6. Quoted in Jennifer Morgan, *Laboring Women, Reproduction and Gender in New World Slavery* (Philadelphia: University of Pennsylvania Press, 2004), 100.

CHAPTER THREE

Enslaved Women in the Revolutionary Era and Early Republic

The ideas that led to the American Revolution and the war itself brought a new perspective on slavery, which eventually led to freedom for slaves in the Northern states. A wave of religious fervor sparked ideas of brotherhood across racial lines and gave rise to discussions about the morality of slavery as a whole. As the colonists spoke against their oppression by the British, many slaves considered the nature of their own oppression. How could the American people reconcile human liberty with the right to own slaves? Slaves recognized that when white men proclaimed "all men are created equal" they did not necessarily mean all men, and they certainly did not mean all women. Yet the Revolution inspired slaves to think about their own liberation, and tens of thousands of bondsmen fought for their freedom on both sides of the conflict, and enslaved women played a vital supporting role. The white men who framed the new constitution of the United States grappled with the issue of slavery, and the eventual compromises they made left the new nation with unresolved issues. Although all Northern states adopted gradual abolition laws after the war, slavery hardened in the South, bringing repercussions for slave women in the years that followed.

In the 1730s, revolutionary ideas about liberty and freedom contributed to the rise of evangelical Protestant Christianity known as the Great Awakening. Following on the heels of the Protestant Reformation, the Enlightenment concept of individual rights led many to question established church hierarchies and to look for more individual, democratic relationships with God. Lay preachers, particularly in the Baptist and Methodist denominations, toured the countryside admonishing sinners to repent and to live lives of morality and Christian charity. Influenced by these calls, many slave owners increasingly believed it was their duty, as good masters, to "educate" their slaves as Christian people, and they actively encouraged baptism for their slaves. As a result, black men and women joined evangelical churches in equal numbers.

Evangelical Christianity was particularly appealing to slaves because it shared certain vocabulary and beliefs with traditional West African practices, including patterns of call and response during worship and a belief in regeneration or rebirth. Baptist and Methodist denominations were both popular with the enslaved as they had relatively loose structures that permitted slaves a degree of freedom in terms of how they worshipped. Moreover, Methodist and Baptist preachers stressed the importance of human worth, dignity, comfort, and hope, all of which resonated with the enslaved. Slave women in particular responded to the evangelical Protestant idea that spiritual authority resulted not from education, social status, or gender but from having experienced the spiritual rebirth or conversion, a belief that had allowed women to play important roles in West African spiritual traditions. Some enslaved women even became lay preachers themselves. Masters soon found they could not simply impose their religious beliefs on their slaves because enslaved people had their own ideas about the type of Christianity they needed. They converted to Christianity because they sought to come to terms with their disrupted lives. They hoped that God would protect their marriages from forced separations. Some women also hoped God would protect them from their masters' lust.

Not all enslaved women converted to Protestant Christianity. Enslaved women embraced a blend of African and new world cultural practices that were adapted to suit the needs of women in bondage seeking hope and optimism for the future. Slaves also underwent a process of "creolization" as they bore children on American soil and the international trade in slaves ended. Enslaved people ceased to be African and became enslaved Americans instead. But some Muslim women fought to maintain their beliefs, although bondage made the continuation of Islamic rituals very difficult. Slaves had no access to the Quran or other religious texts, and their work often made it impossible to pray the required five times per day. Nonetheless, some enslaved women and their descendents tried to maintain other Islamic traditions such as dress style or dietary patterns. Other West African spiritual traditions persisted in the slave quarters. Conjurers who allegedly had magic powers held positions of considerable prestige, and both slaves and white people feared and revered them. Although it was mostly men who performed this role, a few enslaved women were conjurers. Along with midwifery, conjuring represented one of the few opportunities for enslaved women to achieve status and prestige among their peers.

Some of these traditions persisted because the version of Christianity that slave owners presented to their slaves was unattractive. The white ministers who gave sermons to slaves on the plantations often stressed lessons such as "turn the other cheek" and "the meek shall inherit the earth," emphasizing that slaves should not fight back when their masters punished them. The rewards of heaven would be great for those who suffered in silence on this earth, they said. Moreover, blacks were second-class citizens in the white churches. Even when slaves attended with their white masters and mistresses they had to sit at the back or in separate balconies.

Not surprisingly, the Christianity of their owners did not appeal much to enslaved people, who instead developed their own unique forms of Christianity. Many held secret gatherings in the woods or at night to hold their own services. Often they blended African and American traditions such as turning big iron cooking pots upside down at these gatherings, a West African tradition that supposedly prevented white owners from hearing their festivities.

Although most slave preachers were men, religion played a vital and significant part in enslaved women's lives. Women immersed themselves fully in their religious practices and valued their communal aspects. Christmas and Easter were important times, as were life rituals such as baptisms, weddings, and funerals because all provided opportunities for women to break away from their drudgery, catch up with their female friends, indulge in courtship, and pray for future freedom. But whatever form slave women's religion took, their faith mostly remained an "invisible institution." Female slaves kept their religious lives hidden from white owners and worshipped in secret with their peers, even if they attended their masters' churches on Sundays. Nonetheless, in the years that followed the Great Awakening, as war with Britain loomed, enslaved women found their beliefs gave them strength during times of upheaval.

About half a million black people lived in America on the eve of war, representing 20 percent of the total population, but only 5 percent of them were free. While the rise of hostilities affected some enslaved women's lives very little, others played key roles in Patriot protests against the British Crown, voluntarily or not. For example, during the "homespun" campaign, owners forced enslaved women in port cities to spin and weave more cloth following a boycott of imported goods from Britain. Slaves used the rhetoric of independence to boost their own arguments for freedom. Enlightenment ideas of

Benard et Cie, *Phillis Wheatley*. Revue des Colonies 1834–1842. Photographs and Prints Division, Schomburg Center for Research in Black Culture, The New York Public Library, Astor, Lennox and Tilden Foundations.

liberty undoubtedly influenced Phillis Wheatley, an urban enslaved woman who published poems supporting the Patriot cause and freedom for all slaves.

Founding father Thomas Jefferson illustrated the complexities of revolutionary thought. Jefferson's philosophy was typical of Enlightenment thinkers of the time, and the ideas of liberty, tolerance, and republicanism formed the core of modern American thinking. Yet while an early draft of the Declaration of Independence had included a section condemning slavery, he had to withdraw it in order to ensure Southern support for independence. To those who signed the final document, the Declaration's proclamation that all men were entitled to life, liberty, and the pursuit of happiness only applied to white men, not black men, and certainly not enslaved women.

Like many founding fathers, Jefferson held slaves on his Virginia plantation, Monticello. He also famously had a long-term relationship with an enslaved woman, Sally Hemings, who never married and lived her life as his slave. Of the six infants Hemings bore, four survived into adulthood when their father, Jefferson, freed them. Perhaps as a result of Sally's relationship with the master, the Hemings family held important positions on the plantation. Reconciling their broad Enlightenment ideas about freedom and equality with their own personal desires for intimacy with women they held in bondage seems to have posed a great dilemma for some powerful, wealthy, educated slaveholders.

The thirteen colonies began armed conflict against the British in 1775, and they remained at war until 1783 when the Treaty of Paris recognized American independence. As hostilities erupted, enslaved women across the colonies sometimes found themselves alone as their husbands, fathers, and sons joined Rebel or Loyalist forces. In the major Northern cities as a result of men leaving for the war, black women increasingly outnumbered black men, an imbalance that lasted well beyond the revolutionary era. The upheaval of revolution also disrupted the lives of enslaved women living on Southern plantations. White masters left their homes to join in the war effort, often taking male slaves with them, leaving mistresses and slave women to fend for themselves. Like many women in war-torn societies, female slaves found themselves at risk of violence—sexual or otherwise—from soldiers. Soldiers and other roving bands of men sometimes descended upon plantations and farms demanding food and other goods, as well as sexual services from the women. But sometimes war brought positive changes. Many enslaved men and women took advantage of absentee owners and fled from their plantations seeking a new and better life elsewhere, either in the North or in Spanish Florida, a haven for refugee slaves.

Overall, the Revolutionary War offered more opportunities for enslaved men to change their lives than it did slave women. Men had the chance to leave their farms and plantations and fight either for the Rebels or the Loyalists. During the war, many Northern enslaved men fought for local militias because whites promised them their freedom in return. But their wives remained enslaved regardless of their husband's new status. Since they were also less likely to run away than men, enslaved women's lives in wartime were often characterized by continuity more than change.

The actions of the British authorities furthered the issue of freedom, however. In 1775, the British governor of Virginia, Earl Dunmore, issued a proclamation promising freedom to any enslaved man who joined the Loyalists. Many slave men took this opportunity to flee their owners. Meanwhile, in

1777, as slaves began to flock to the British forces, General George Washington authorized slaves to fight in the Continental Army in exchange for their freedom. Soon, the number of slaves running to the British forces declined. Enslaved men who fought with the Loyalists began to fear Rebel retaliation against their families who remained on the plantations. The British also hired thirty thousand mercenaries, which made black soldiers less vital.

However, the British recognized the economic importance of slavery to the Rebels and decided to expand Dunmore's policy. In 1779, the British commander in chief, General Sir Henry Clinton, offered any slave the chance to join the British with the implied promise of freedom in return. Following this proclamation, thousands of slave men, women, and children joined the British effort, growing food on plantations for the troops or working as their servants or laborers. Although Clinton's Proclamation offered enslaved women a chance to gain their freedom, the day-to-day nature of their labor barely changed. Female slaves continued to perform strenuous outdoor field labor as well as "women's work" laboring as houseservants, cooks, laundresses, and maids. They had only meager food supplies, scant clothing and other provisions, and some women also had to contend with the wartime deaths of their loved ones.

Thus, both sides promised some slaves their freedom in exchange for fighting, but for strategic purposes rather than humanitarian concerns about slavery itself. Moreover, slave men and women did not define themselves as either Patriots or Loyalists for ideological reasons because such terms were largely meaningless for enslaved people. Instead, they pragmatically transformed the conflict into a war of liberation by serving in the military in exchange for their freedom or by taking advantage of the chaos to run away.

Some enslaved women in the North turned to the law rather than the military or their masters in their attempts to gain their freedom. For example, in 1781, a black Massachusetts woman named Elizabeth, or "Mum Bett," with the assistance of attorney Theodore Sedgwick, claimed her freedom in the courts, insisting that the state's constitution declared "all men are born free and equal." She later became a paid servant in Sedgwick's household and adopted the new name of Elizabeth Freeman. In 1783, after Massachusetts abolished slavery, another black woman petitioned the state legislature demanding "back pay" for her labor as a slave. Belinda complained that her former master had denied her even "one morsel" of his "immense wealth, a part whereof hath been accumulated by her own industry."[1] The legislature agreed, and paid Belinda an annual pension drawn from the rent acquired by her former owner renting out his home.

Between 1777 and 1804 all Northern states abolished slavery. In addition, some slaveholders independently freed their slaves, or allowed them to purchase their freedom. By 1810, the free black population of the North had grown from only several hundred in the 1770s to nearly fifty thousand. However, for Northern black women, the process of gradual emancipation was too slow. Gradual abolition laws stipulated that males born into slavery had to serve their master as "apprentices" until they reached the age of twenty-one or even twenty-eight years old. Females born in bondage gained freedom between the ages of twenty-one to twenty-five. Vermont was the only state to abolish slavery outright in its constitution. In 1810, twenty-seven thousand slaves still remained in the Northern states of the United States. Isabella Baumfree was one such slave. Born in rural New York in 1797, she managed to negotiate her freedom from her Dutch owners in 1826, one year before the state of New York liberated all bondspeople born before 1799. Isabella changed her name to Sojourner Truth in 1843 when her religious convictions led to her involvement in abolitionism and the early women's rights movements. She became an important campaigner and lecturer in both the suffragist and antislavery causes.

Over time, black women in the Northern states gradually gained their freedom, even as many women rapidly learned that racial discrimination and poverty remained a presence in their everyday lives. Women eked out a subsistence standard of living in the urban and rural North just as they had done as slaves. Meanwhile, as slavery grew ever more entrenched in the South, it became a regional issue, a "peculiar institution" that would eventually wrench the new United States in two.

The U.S. Constitution ratified in 1789 also affected enslaved women. Despite antislavery sentiment among the Northern delegates, the new American government did not abolish slavery and denied all black people legal citizenship. Bitter divisions among the founders of the new nation led to the introduction of constitutional clauses designed to compromise between proslavery and antislavery advocates. The Constitution recognized slaves as three-fifths of a white person for the purposes of political representation. The new federal government also agreed to permit the continuation of the African trade in slaves until at least 1808 so long as it reserved the right to levy taxes on imported Africans. Lastly, Article IV of the Constitution included a fugitive slave clause requiring the return of runaway slaves to their owners. Congress passed the Fugitive Slave act in 1793 to implement this clause, although the Act was weakly enforced. The prospect of the end of the international slave trade encouraged slaveholders to increasingly see the value of their female slaves as reproducers as well as laborers, and masters now had a real vested interest in seeing their chattel bear offspring. Moreover, the actual closing of the international trade in 1808 resulted in the replacement of the transatlantic trade with a thriving domestic trade in people, as more and more states entered the Union and America expanded westward over the course of the nineteenth century.

Antislavery advocates gained a small victory with the passage of the Northwest Ordinance in 1789, which organized the additional land that the United States had gained as a result of the peace treaty with Britain into the Northwest Territory and established guidelines for the admission of new states to the Union. The ordinance prohibited slavery in the new territory, establishing the Ohio River as a boundary between the slave states of the South and the free states of the North. The ordinance affected enslaved women indirectly, but significantly. In fostering a geographic division between those parts of America that held slaves and those that were free, the American government facilitated one crucial form of enslaved resistance: escape to the North. But running away from slavery to the Northern states was difficult, so it was mostly enslaved men who escaped, not women.

The question over whether new states should be admitted to the Union as slave or free led to ongoing national debates. The Louisiana Purchase of 1803 gave the United States 828,000 square miles of former French territory that then had to be organized into slave and free states. Likewise, the American acquisition of Florida from Spain in 1819 created an opportunity for slavery's expansion South, and also for owners to reclaim fugitive slaves who had fled to safety when it was under Spanish control.

In South Carolina, international events had unexpected consequences for enslaved women. The slave rebellion in Haiti (1791–1803) led to a vast influx of black and white refugees from the island into the state. The Haitians' mingling with Charleston's urban slaves unnerved the area's slaveholders who increasingly worried about possible rebellion in their own city. So South Carolina legislators, followed by those in the rest of the South, gradually moved to restrict the manumission of slaves, fearing free people of color were more likely to incite revolt among their chattel. This change adversely affected enslaved women, who had more often been the beneficiaries of manumission in the colonial era, often as a result of intimate relationships with their masters.

Economic as well as political developments affected the lives of enslaved women. Eli Whitney's invention of a mechanical cotton gin in 1794 raised the amount of profit owners could extract from their male and female chattel because the gin separated cotton fibers from seeds quickly and efficiently. Moreover, the need for cotton in the industrializing societies of Western Europe created ever more demand for the crop. By the beginning of the nineteenth century, slaveholders expected that their enslaved women both work harder to grant their masters more profits through the value of their labor and reproduce quicker to enable their masters to profit from the value of their offspring. Enslaved women's dual exploitation grew ever more entrenched with detrimental effects on slave women's physical and mental health as they endured multiple pregnancies and forced separation from beloved families and friends.

Many female slaves endured very poor physical health, although their white owners often dismissed their concerns, believing instead that women mostly pretended to be sick to escape work. But medical historians have shown that frequent pregnancies and childbirth adversely affected the health of enslaved women who were weakened by the physical demands of forced labor and inadequate diets. Slaves' diets lacked enough protein, fruits, and vegetables unless the slaves themselves supplemented them by growing produce in their gardens or patches, or by hunting and fishing. Like enslaved men, as a result of their poor living and working conditions, slave women also could suffer from pneumonia, diarrhea, smallpox, cholera, blindness, sore eyes, skin irritations, rickets, scurvy, backache, and toothache. Even when these afflictions did not result in death, they caused significant discomfort.

Following the closing of the international slave trade in 1808, a thriving domestic slave trade emerged, and so masters increasingly encouraged their female slaves to produce more children. More frequent childbirth endangered the lives of both mothers and their infants. Female slaves tended to give birth to their first child at age nineteen, two years younger than white Southern women. Most then had a child every two-and-a-half years thereafter, normally until their mid to late thirties, although not all children survived. White masters professed that black women were promiscuous and highly fertile, but since the slaveholders were the direct beneficiaries of female slaves giving birth, they encouraged a large number of children. They offered various "incentives" to give birth, including reduced workloads, more substantial food allocations, better quality clothing, and larger housing, many of which the women gratefully received. However, owners' enforced breeding of slaves was a relatively rare occurrence. Masters sometimes attempted to persuade or otherwise cajole enslaved women into marrying men they considered a "suitable" match. But it was easier for masters to permit their slave women to marry a man of their own choosing and hope that many valuable children would result than to force them to "pair up" with someone against their will. Thus, enslaved women had value as workers, but it was as reproducers that they generated vast profits for masters by increasing their supply of chattel.

Despite an increasing involvement of medical professionals during labor by the mid-nineteenth century, many female slaves largely relied on the practical and emotional support of enslaved midwives, known as grannies. Neonatal tetanus (lockjaw), caused by bacteria generated by improper handling of umbilical cords, was common among newborn infants. Mothers, too, frequently suffered from postpartum fevers caused by a lack of basic hygiene during birth. They endured mastitis, or inflamed breast tissue, when breast-feeding their infants, and overall fatigue was commonplace.

Other sicknesses and problems associated with pregnancy and childbirth included the retention of placentas, breech births, ectopic pregnancies, and premature labor. Frequent pregnancies also caused slave women's wombs to prolapse, while others suffered from tears and fissures. Problems of the womb, bladder, and bowel forever plagued some mothers. Women's reproductive cycles also caused them considerable health-related problems aside from the monthly annoyance of menstrual pain. Tumors and fibroids led to excessive and uncomfortable bleeding between cycles or overly heavy menstrual flow that was hard to cope with in a hygienic manner and that often led to infection. Some malnourished and overworked slaves had irregular or interrupted menstrual cycles. Enslaved women only survived these ordeals through the practical support, advice, and companionship of their fellow female slaves who assisted with the birthing of children; who tended sore, lactating breasts; washed menstrual rags; and who doctored female ailments using traditional remedies and cures.

Slave women used their knowledge of roots and herbs to cure sickness throughout their enslavement. Sometimes their knowledge converged with magical or spiritual beliefs to create unique cultural patterns; for example, when female "root doctors" made herbal remedies to cure the sick. Solomon Caldwell remembered his mother making various herbal medicines, including a tea made from grass to ward off fever, and another for "chills" made from elder twigs and dogwood berries. Caldwell's mother probably obtained her knowledge from her own elders.

More rarely, some may have used their knowledge of roots and herbs to poison their white owners. While it is impossible to calculate how often enslaved women poisoned their white masters, mistresses, or other family members, it is clear that slave owners thought it a possibility. Poisoning was particularly suited to enslaved women because the sexual division of labor dictated they should serve as plantation cooks and nurses. Invoking white fears empowered female slaves and senior women, including root doctors and midwives, occupied positions of high social standing in slave quarters. Slaveowners often assumed that they alone awarded slaves social status by granting some women more "prestigious" jobs than others. But enslaved men and women created their own social hierarchies that rewarded women and men who helped others.

Enslaved women also used their plant lore outside the realm of medicine. Continuing the practices of their African forebears, they dyed their clothes in vibrant colors that were often at odds with white people's notions of "appropriate" taste for enslaved people. Rejecting the subjugation of their enslavement through their dress, female slaves often enjoyed raising the ire of their mistresses and masters though their vivid and flamboyant clothes. They mixed bright colors in ways unfamiliar to white Americans with European heritage, who regarded the bright colors as merely "clashing." These cheery clothes provided shared moments of happiness, excitement, and joy in enslaved women's otherwise dull and monotonous lives. Communal activities such as clothes dying also enabled enslaved women to develop friendships and support networks within a female sphere based upon mutual interests.

Women's activities in the early republic commonly provided a link back to African pasts and female ancestors at a time when cultural memories remained strong. Following the cultural traditions their mothers and grandmothers taught them, enslaved women linked the old world and the new. They adapted African traditions to their lives as American slaves, thus making their own important cultural contribution to the United States and its history. For example, traditional West African patterns influenced the food, utensils, and cooking styles of "Gullah"—named for the unique regional linguistic style among slaves in the South Carolina and Georgia lowcountry. Typically, Gullah women cooked spicy food communally over large, open fireplaces, allowing them to socialize while maintaining elements of their ancestors' traditions.

But despite their contributions to creating communities and families, given their legal status as chattel, slave women could not always keep them intact. The forced separation of enslaved women from their families, friends, and communities took a number of forms. The most dreaded possibility in the early republic was to be sold to a long-distance trader who would drive them west in a chain gang before selling them "down the river" to Alabama, Mississippi, and Louisiana. Typically, these traders shackled slaves together into a long "coffle" of between forty and one hundred slaves chained together. Traders were more likely to shackle men than women, believing men were more likely to run away. Instead, they tied women with ropes or leather, and sometimes they let pregnant women ride on carts with young children. However, this division of slaves according to sex had important consequences for enslaved women: isolated from black men, they were vulnerable to sexual assault at the hands of their traders, just as their predecessors had faced sexual abuse on the slave ships crossing the Atlantic. An 1819 image of a slave coffle in Washington, D.C., shows men chained at the front, while a woman walks freely at the back with her child.

Forced separations affected enslaved women to varying degrees. In some instances, slaveholders uprooted their families and chattel and moved westward in the hope of making larger profits in the fertile, virgin soil of new American lands. Such migrations had only a limited impact on slave women's personal relationships if their families belonged to the same master. However, when their husbands belonged to different masters, separations were permanent. Most enslaved women considered themselves to be very lucky when their owners sold them in a "gang" alongside their spouses and

Slave Coffle, Washington, D.C., ca. 1819, in William Cullen Bryant and Sidney Howard Gay, *A Popular History of the United States, vol. 4* (New York, 1881), 266. Library of Congress, Prints and Photographs Division, LC-USZ62-2574.

children, although owners did not parcel their slaves for reasons of compassion but because they could "sneak" elderly or disabled chattel into gangs and rid themselves of people they considered a burden. Some owners sold their female slaves to nearby plantations, while others simply hired them out to local white families. These women, either domestics or fieldworkers, could be parted from their families for just a few months or for a year, but they could often maintain their familial relationships following separation. However, victims of the long-distance trade had no option but to regard their separations from family and friends with a painful sense of permanency. Other enslaved women and girls became separated from their loved ones upon the death of their owner, or because white people gave them away as gifts; for example, for a white child's birthday or upon marriage.

The domestic slave trade broke up approximately one-third of slave marriages and separated one-fifth of enslaved children from their parents. Owners were more likely to sell men in single lots than women, whom they sometimes sold with children to serve as caretakers. But even when owners did not sell or separate families, all slaves lived under a cloud of fear about possible future separations, and all knew of slaves who had been forcibly wrenched apart from their loved ones. The widespread sale and separation of beloved family members represents one of the cruelest blows of slavery.

Slave purchases involved important economic considerations for owners. White men looked for certain characteristics when buying female slaves. They wanted strong, fit, and healthy-looking women, especially after 1808 when, apart from a small illegal trade, slave imports no longer arrived from Africa and it became ever more important for owners to have their enslaved population reproduce. But despite women's value as potential mothers, slaveholders still placed a higher monetary value on enslaved men. Men and women both reached their maximum values between the ages of twenty-one and twenty-five, after which women's value declined, while men's remained high until they reached the age of thirty-five. So enslaved women's fertility affected their monetary value, with younger female slaves commanding the highest prices. A notice (p. 54) makes a point of mentioning the young age of a female houseservant and seamstress as an incentive for purchase. In contrast, slave men, whose primary worth was as workers, retained their value into their thirties.

The reality of being sold on an auction block to the highest bidder was brutal. Throughout the South, potential owners poked and prodded black women, subjecting them to cruel, intrusive physical examination of their mouths, breasts, and genitalia to try to gauge their ages and whether they might have borne children. Sellers buffed and polished their chattels' skin,

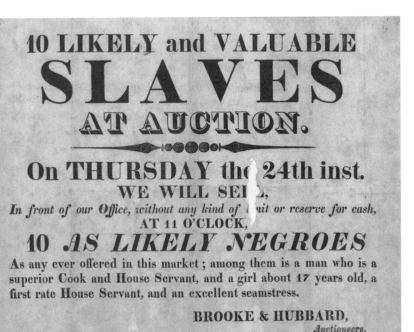

Notice of Slave Auction, Richmond, Virginia, 1823. Chicago History Museum.

oiled their hair, and dressed them well in order to get the maximum price. Some white men had highly sinister motivations for purchasing female slaves. They bought only young, attractive, typically light-skinned women to trade as "fancy girls" for white men who desired sexual relationships with them.

White slaveholders of the revolutionary era and the early republic created a system of bondage in the Southern United States that extracted the maximum value from enslaved women. They forced women into arduous labor in the fields or as domestics, and they brutally punished those whose labor was not up to par, who rebelled against their oppression, or who rejected white men's sexual advances. Subjected to violent assaults, sexual or otherwise, enslaved women had little respite from the onslaughts of bondage. At the same time, white owners also exploited their female slaves as reproducers of valuable chattel. Enslaved women struggled to cope with the dual demands of work and childrearing, and they found little sympathy from their privileged white mistresses who frequently regarded their enslaved women with hostility, anger, rage, or misplaced jealousy.

Overall, despite the promises of equality of the Great Awakening and revolutionary ideology, the daily lives of most female slaves changed little during the American Revolution. Although many Northern enslaved women gained their freedom, political and economic considerations cemented slavery in the South in the new republic. Racial lines and enslavement grew more rigid and more entrenched in the South, and the end of the international slave trade and Northern emancipation had devastating implications for women held in bondage. While still valued as laborers, masters increasingly viewed slave women's roles as reproducers as equally important. Meanwhile, slave women themselves maintained what cultural traditions they could and tried to maintain a sense of community in the slave quarters even in the face of the ever-present threat of separation.

Note

1. Quoted in Douglas R. Egerton, *Death or Liberty: African Americans and Revolutionary America* (Oxford and New York: Oxford University Press, 2009), 104–5, 109.

CHAPTER FOUR

Enslaved Women in the Antebellum South

Following the end of the international slave trade in 1808, some Americans expected slavery to slowly wither away. They were wrong. Although it was no longer a national institution, slavery became further entrenched in the South during the antebellum era, with a thriving domestic slave trade replacing the Atlantic trade. The number of slaves increased from around 698,000 in 1790 to almost four million in 1860. Enslaved women became especially valuable to slaveholders, as they could both labor and reproduce. Women took on a variety of different roles depending on their stage of life. Daughters', wives', mothers', and grandmothers' experiences all varied, but their gender shaped the basic patterns of their lives in similar ways. Nonetheless, through their everyday family lives, enslaved women, with spousal support, female friendships, and their own skills, created a degree of "social space" or psychological distance from their white owners.

As reproducers, female slaves stood at the heart of the increase in the enslaved population because frequent childbearing generated a rising future supply of slaves for their masters. In most states, male slaves constituted the majority of enslaved people, reflecting their desirability as workers. But the number of states with a female slave majority rose from two in 1820 to five in 1840, and to six in 1860 (Table 4.1). The immense profits generated from the domestic slave trade, as well as the products of slave labor, grew ever larger in antebellum times.

Moreover, women also had great value as laborers. Arduous fieldwork characterized the lives of most female slaves. The gang and task systems continued in the antebellum period. Field women working on plantations under

Table 4.1.   Numbers of Enslaved Men and Women by State, 1820–1860

State	1820 Men/Women	1840 Men/Women	1860 Men/Women
Alabama	19,147/22,732	127,360/126,172	217,766/217,314
Arkansas	N/A / N/A	10,119/9,816	56,174/54,941
Delaware	2,555/1,954	1,371/1,234	860/938
Florida	N/A / N/A	12,748/12,679	31,348/30,397
Georgia	75,914/73,740	139,335/141,609	229,193/233,005
Kentucky	63,914/62,818	91,004/91,254	113,015/112,474
Louisiana	36,116/32,948	86,529/81,923	171,977/159,749
Maryland	56,372/51,025	46,201/43,536	44,313/42,876
Mississippi	16,850/15,964	98,003/97,208	219,301/217,330
Missouri	5,341/4,881	28,742/29,498	57,360/57,571
North Carolina	106,605/98,466	123,546/122,271	166,469/164,590
South Carolina	133,807/124,668	158,678/168,360	196,571/205,835
Tennessee	39,747/40,360	91,477/91,582	136,370/139,349
Texas	N/A / N/A	N/A /29,461	91,229/91,337
Virginia	218,274/206,879	228,661/220,426	249,483/241,382
Total numbers of enslaved men and women (including a minority in the Northern states)	**866,547/671,491**	**1,249,302/1,238,153**	**1,984,620/1,969,140**

Figures taken from Ira Berlin, *Generations of Captivity*, appendix 1, and Daina Ramey Berry, *Enslaved Women in America: An Encyclopedia* (Santa Barbara, CA: AeC-Cliol Greenwood, 2012), appendix.

the gang system labored under the supervision of men, either white overseers or black drivers, employed to ensure slaves worked as hard as they possibly could, with physical force if necessary. As in colonial times, overseers and drivers could be cruel and brutal. While some former slaves remembered compassion from those black drivers who tried to spare them the whip, others recalled violent whippings and beatings at the hands of black men in positions of authority. Former slaves also remembered horrific sexual assaults by men in positions of power, especially white overseers, although women were often reluctant to divulge such intimate information to white interviewers. South Carolinian Gus Feaster said his white overseer was "a wicked man. He take 'vantage of all de slaves when he git half chance."[1] Minnie Fulkes also described the dreadful physical abuse inflicted on her mother by a white overseer because she refused to consent to a sexual relationship with him.

Fieldwork, even when not dangerous, was also monotonous for slave women. In contrast to enslaved men, who had many opportunities to achieve positions of status and prestige on plantations—as drivers, carriage men, butlers, carpenters, tanners, blacksmiths, and other skilled artisans—most female slaves were tied to their plantations on an everyday basis. Although restrictive legislation slowly decreased the geographic mobility of all slaves during the antebellum era, skilled men met more people and spent at least some of their time socializing away from the slave quarters. Enslaved women, however, remained stifled by their geographic constraints. Enslaved field men had more opportunities to vary their workload and to acquire status through their work—opportunities never granted to enslaved women.

But despite the risk of brutal punishments by drivers or overseers, the everyday monotony, and the backbreaking arduousness of field labor, most enslaved women still preferred this kind of work to laboring for owners in their "Big House." Women forged friendships in the fields with their fellow slaves with whom they talked and sang. Being located away from their white owners also gave enslaved women a valuable sense of space, despite the ongoing threat of physical or sexual assault by men. Nonetheless, female slaves' strenuous field labor was at odds with idealized contemporary notions of femininity exemplified by the white Southern "lady." Wealthy white women were supposed to be chaste and pure, unsullied by the drudgery and dirt of everyday life. Such notions of "proper" white womanhood dictated that ladies should live a life of refined leisure pursuits and genteel activities. But rich white women were only able to devote their lives to such refined pleasures through the labor of their black enslaved women who performed all their chores for them. Deemed physically and mentally inferior to black and white men, and "unfeminine" because of their race, female slaves were exploited for both their alleged physical strength and their abilities as women to bear children. Such were the contradictory images of their role in society.

Not all female slaves plowed, planted, and gathered in the fields. Enslaved children were generally spared from work until they reached the age of five. Thereafter, young girls performed light tasks on the plantation, including picking up litter, tidying, and sweeping. Some young girls formed part of plantation "trash gangs" along with elderly, injured, or sickly slaves who were physically incapable of fieldwork. Because owners considered all female slaves to be suitable "caregivers," they put some girls in charge of younger children, or granted them the role of "playmate" to young white children. Some former slaves had fond memories of childhood friendships with young whites. Millie Sampson recalled playing with white children and learning new words from them. But these friendships often fell apart as both parties gained an awareness of the significance of racial difference. One eleven-year-old enslaved girl protested having to refer to a baby as "young mistress."

Upon reaching adolescence, one-quarter of all slave girls moved into the Big House of their owners to labor as domestic servants. This brought its own unique set of circumstances and combination of benefits and pressures for enslaved women just as it had in colonial times. House slaves were spared the everyday hardships of a life outdoors in the hot fields because owners ensured their often luxurious homes were shaded, cool, and comfortable for the white inhabitants. House labor itself was also considerably more varied than fieldwork. Owners mostly employed younger, less-skilled slave girls as general house servants while more mature and experienced women worked as cooks, laundresses, seamstresses, and nannies. Lactating women sometimes served as wet nurses for young white children. Some of their work in the Big House, unlike field labor, gave enslaved women real opportunities to acquire status and prestige in the eyes of whites. Former slave Louisa Davis remembered her mother running the plantation kitchen as a "mammy" figure, and in return her white owners permitted her to eat the same meals as they did.

A strong and influential female slave, mammy oversaw the everyday running of the Big House. White people developed a stereotype of mammy that was testament to a positive depiction of proslavery ideology, as the image on page 61 conveys. For whites, the mammy represented all that was good about slavery. Loyal and devoted, mammy was "in charge" of domestic life in the Big House. From the perspective of the slave quarters, running the everyday life of a white household required strategy, energy, careful planning, and initiative. The mammy therefore held status among her enslaved peers as well as white owners.

While their work may have been more varied, women laboring in the relative isolation of the Big House missed out on the everyday camaraderie and supportive environment that the field slaves created. Domestic servants remained at the beck and call of white men and women, sometimes twenty-four hours a day. Jessie Sparrow remembered having to sleep on a wooden pallet at the end of her mistress's bed at night. There was no respite at the end of Sparrow's hard working day and no private space to where she could retreat from demanding whites. And close proximity to white men of the Big House also rendered female slaves at high risk of sexual assault and other forms of physical cruelty.

Enslaved women were uniquely subjected to a triple exploitation, as black people, as slaves, and as women. And nowhere was this exploitation clearer than in the realm of enslaved women's work. Enslaved women were often given "extra" tasks to perform for their masters and mistresses due to ideas of divisions of labor by gender. Slaveholder Thomas Blewett kept his slaves out of the fields on rainy days, but while his enslaved men earned a day's respite,

Female Cook in Her Kitchen, Early 1850s. Harper's New Monthly Magazine, 12 (January 1856), 177. AP2.H3. Special Collections, University of Virginia, Charlottesville, VA.

female slaves had to make clothes. Plantation mistress Margaret Anne Morris decreed that her enslaved women had to make clothes in the evenings after their arduous work in the fields was over, while other female slaves had to spin or weave late into the night to perform their work obligations. Former slave Genia Woodberry remembered enslaved women carrying large cooking pots to the field on her South Carolina plantation. These women then prepared everyone's food in addition to performing their own field labor.

But it was not only white people who assigned enslaved women extra work to do at the end of their exhausting working day. Enslaved men assumed their wives, mothers, and daughters would perform the bulk of domestic chores within their family cabins, including cleaning, cooking, washing, tidying, and taking care of children. The great burden of this domestic labor fell to slave women, while men enjoyed more sociable and interesting domestic chores that often took them away from the quarters, such as hunting and fishing or tending to their plots of land or vegetable patches at the end of the working day or on weekends. Yet women could sometimes find satisfaction in this work. Along the coastal sea islands of South Carolina and Georgia, enslaved women and their descendants gained a reputation as skilled artisans of high-quality basketware made from seagrass. However, during the antebellum era they found it harder to sell their goods at local markets than did colonial women because Southern states increasingly imposed restrictions on the geographic mobility of slaves. Other slave women made beautiful patchwork quilts from scraps of fabric. Ex-slave Fannie Moore remembered her mother quilting at night, and Camilla Jackson recalled groups of enslaved women quilting at the end of their long and arduous workday. Women visited each other's cabins, quilting, and chatting, until everyone had sufficient bedding for the winter. Communal quilting provided occasions for women to chat, gossip, and share advice. More importantly, it provided them with an important sense of friendship and camaraderie that existed alongside supportive relationships with husbands, parents, and children.

Before most other women in American society, female slaves pioneered the demanding "double day" of work. They labored for someone else during daylight hours and for their families after sunset. Coupled with the frequent bearing and rearing of children, enslaved women's lives were often characterized by sheer exhaustion. Former slave Maggie Wright recalled how masters expected enslaved mothers to work all day after they had been awake most of the night tending to their babies. Greenville mistress Elizabeth Franklin Perry described in a letter to her husband, Benjamin, how she was unhappy with her slave Eliza, whose family always had "dirty clothes." When Mrs. Perry scolded Eliza for not being a better housekeeper, or for not sewing the cloth she had provided into clothes for her family, Eliza replied:

> She had no time to work for herself, that she could not see to wash at night, her eyes were bad, and after getting her supper and putting her children to sleep, there was very little time until nine o'clock, the time . . . she must go to bed, and after working all day steadily for me, she was not able to work at night.[2]

Eliza was not alone in struggling to meet the demands of being a slave laborer, a wife, and a mother.

While enslaved women's roles within their families and broader communities involved a great deal of hard work, at other times, especially for young girls, community life brought moments of great joy. Women played roles in a wide variety of social events such as weekend dances, corn-shucking parties, and quilting bees. White ownership obviously severely curtailed the ability of enslaved women to live their lives as they desired, but female slaves nonetheless carved out a modicum of independence for themselves to varying degrees, and through their own initiative women were able to survive and to resist the onslaught of the regime.

Most slave girls grew up expecting to marry and looked forward to finding a spouse. They knew from an early age that owners expected marriage and children because slave babies increased their supply of chattel. But enslaved girls also wanted to enter wedlock and bear children for themselves because marriage and offspring brought personal happiness. Female support networks were also vitally important for enslaved women, but these existed alongside, rather than in competition with, the romantic associations between women and men and the parental bonds between mothers and children. Occasionally female slaves had voluntary intimate relationships with white men, while others were romantically attached to free men of color. However, most slave women met and married slave men, with whom they survived slavery as a loving partnership. Young men and women enjoyed courtship rituals as well as Saturday night dances or parties, which provided important respite after the hardships of the working week. Owners sometimes attempted to control these events. For example, some masters regulated attendance at dances by restricting the number of passes they distributed or by attending themselves. Others refused point blank to allow their slaves to attend dances on other plantations, sometimes simply to assert their authority. But their slaves—both male and female—fought back by holding "secret" dances or religious meetings, and in doing so, enslaved women carved out a degree of independence from whites in their social lives between "sundown and sunup."

Illicit gatherings were especially important for enslaved women because they had fewer legitimate opportunities to leave their plantations than men. But despite being more confined to their quarters than their male counterparts, enslaved women challenged their geographic containment. They left their sanctioned quarters illicitly under cover of darkness to socialize with other women, to meet men, to worship God, or simply to dance and celebrate on their own terms far away from prying and scolding white masters and mistresses. The great majority of enslaved women met their spouses at Saturday night dances, whether owners sanctioned such events or not.

In both enslaved and white society, men initiated courtship rituals, while women assumed more passive roles. These clearly defined gendered roles created among the enslaved provided opportunities for masculine and feminine self-expression that bondage all too often threatened. Slave men felt empowered by their active role in courtship, in contrast to their working week, when they were subject to the control (and sometimes the brutality) of their master or overseer. Former slave George Fleming recalled specific dances such as "please and displease" and "hack-back." Teenage boys and girls had to face each other and dance back and forth, and the girls had to ask the boys what would please them. The boys retorted "a kiss frum dat purty gal over dar."[3] Likewise, Gus Feaster remembered young slave women hiding honeysuckle and rose petals in their clothes during dances. Courtship constituted pleasurable and memorable times for all slaves, providing romantic excitement amid the monotony of bondage. Because the cultural lives of many enslaved women usually revolved around some form of labor—be this making quilts, baskets, or other goods; or spinning, sewing, repairing, or making clothes—the chance to gain some respite from work, to worship God, sing, dance, and enjoy oneself was of particular importance. Saturday night dances offered enslaved women a chance to forget about the working week and the chores to be completed at home and to partake in pleasurable, exciting activities. Women dressed up and styled their hair. They prayed, danced, listened to music, sang, courted with the opposite sex, and listened to stories.

Yet women perhaps experienced these social events less freely than men. Preachers who assumed leadership roles tended to be male. More men than women played musical instruments such as fiddles or took the initiative in courtship rituals. Men, not women, held court while telling stories and leading the communal singing or praying. Men expected to charm slave women, and the latter played less active roles in community celebrations. However, this did not necessarily mitigate women's enjoyment of social events; it meant their experiences, like their lives as a whole, were shaped through the prism of their gender.

Courtship led most young couples toward marriage. Despite white owners scant regard for the legitimacy of their slaves' marriages, they themselves often played a role in slave weddings, even though, as property, enslaved people could not legally wed under American law. However, custom and notions of paternalism overrode the rule of law. White masters and mistresses liked to believe they had their slaves' "best interests" at heart, and they sometimes permitted slave weddings to be important, lavish affairs. Enslaved women often got married in their owners' Big House, wearing a full wedding dress, while white family members gave gifts to the couple and provided a feast. White ministers or masters performed the ceremonies for some enslaved women, while others had black preachers to legitimize slave unions according to Christian faith. Enslaved couples often partook in a symbolic ritual of jumping over a broom to symbolize their newfound wedlock, a tradition harking back to preindustrial English society. They danced afterward, and slaves continued their own celebrations long after their white owners' departure. For young enslaved women, wedding ceremonies constituted an important rite of passage on route to womanhood, an event they looked forward to with excitement and enthusiasm. These all-too-few moments of sheer joy eclipsed memories of life's drudgery and monotony for many enslaved women.

Following their weddings, enslaved wives found that the love and support of their spouses helped provide a shield against the oppression of bondage, although wedlock also placed enslaved spouses at risk of future agony should they be forcibly separated. And marriage caused other anguishes as well. Enslaved men and women witnessed one another's brutal physical punishment, and men sometimes saw white men sexually assault their wives. Enslaved couples regarded wedlock and their marital vows with the utmost seriousness, which made the wrenching apart of their marriages by slaveholders all the more callous. Perhaps the sentiments of Susan Hamlin, an antebellum slave from Charleston, South Carolina, exemplify well how many enslaved women must have felt about enforced separations. She poignantly described how "all time, night an' day, you could hear men an' women screamin' to de tip of dere voices as either pa, ma, sister, or brother, was take without any warning an' sell. Sometime mother who had only one chile was separated fur life. People wus always dyin' frum a broken heart."[4]

But despite these risks, most enslaved women still desired to love and marry. Indeed, unlike many members of white society, who married for reasons of property and pragmatism, the enslaved, for whom "property" had little relevance, were early pioneers in entering wedlock purely for reasons of romantic love. Sometimes slave marriage angered masters, especially when enslaved women they coveted for themselves displayed affection for another man. "I'll soon convince you whether I am your master, or the nigger fellow you honor so highly," thundered "Dr. Flint" to "Linda Brendt," "Harriet Jacob" (James Norcom). "If you *must* have a husband you may take up with one of my slaves." But Harriet was in love with a free black carpenter, whom she wanted to marry. "Don't you suppose sir," she replied, "that slaves can have some preference about marrying? Do you suppose that all men are alike to her?"[5]

Some married slave women lived apart from their husbands during the week because they belonged to different owners. Only those living on fairly large plantations could enter wedlock with someone belonging to the same master. Some wealthy slaveholders who owned many slaves, such as the lowcountry planter Charles Manigault, simply prohibited cross-plantation, or abroad, marriages. "I allow no strange negro to take a wife on my place" he wrote, in typically patriarchal prose that assumed enslaved women's subservience.[6] Planters such as Manigault considered cross-plantation marriages highly risky because they took slaves away from their plantations to visit loved ones, permitted slaves to see a wider world and different ways of life, and created opportunities to run away or question the regime. But even within South Carolina, where large plantations were relatively plentiful, around one-third of all enslaved marriages crossed plantations because enslaved men and women fought to wed someone of their own choosing, even though this type of matrimony at times complicated women's marital life. Slave women who married men living on other plantations had to spend the bulk of the working week away from their husbands. Sometimes they shared cabins with lodgers, all the time laboring for their owners and caring for their children without spousal assistance. Masters also regarded women in abroad unions as essentially "single" for most of the time, rendering them more at risk of sexual assault than women whose husbands were present. Thus, for enslaved women with abroad husbands, the help and support of other female slaves during the working week, including mothers, sisters, aunts, and friends, proved to be invaluable.

Enslaved women in cross-plantation marriages had to be especially strong and resourceful. Most saw their husbands only on weekends, when gendered conventions among slaves and whites dictated that enslaved husbands, not wives, did the visiting. Mattie Jackson, enslaved in Missouri, described in her autobiography how her parents maintained their "abroad" marriage after her mother was sold some twenty miles away. Her father visited once a week, undertaking the long walk on a Saturday evening and returning on a Sunday night. But later in Jackson's life her father was sold westward, and she never saw him again. Some husbands, who walked many miles to see their abroad wives, did so with a written pass from their owners. Yet others risked illicit spousal visits without a pass, hoping they would not be caught and punished by white patrollers and their vicious dogs. Slave women remained bound to their homes much more than men, partly because of women's child-rearing responsibilities, but also because more men partook in labor that took them beyond the immediate confines of their plantation or quarters. Nor did enslaved husbands expect their wives to visit them elsewhere because they considered traveling away from quarters highly risky. Enslaved women beyond their farms and plantations aroused white suspicions. Female slaves, therefore, lived in a narrower, more restricted world than men.

Owners frequently interfered in their slaves' romantic affairs, attempting to influence courtship, marital partners, and spousal living arrangements. This interference in the everyday lives of their female slaves meant enslaved wives often had to find innovative responses to forced sales and separations that took family members, including spouses and children, away. Sometimes they lived with extended families with stepparents, grandparents, or other networks, including so-called fictive or "swap-dog" kin, who performed chores that abroad spouses would normally do, assuming that similar "kin" helped their family members on other plantations. Some women, especially those in abroad marriages, took in lodgers whose wives often belonged to different owners and were forced to live apart during the workweek. For example, Charles Ball described in his autobiography how after being separated from his wife and children he lodged with another enslaved family. On weekends men left their lodgings to spend time with their wives elsewhere, while women welcomed their own abroad husbands into their cabins.

While some enslaved women lived in a system of abroad wedlock, others were able to share a cabin with their husbands permanently. These marriages were somewhat easier for enslaved women since men were on hand to help with the day-to-day burdens of laboring for masters in addition to carrying out domestic chores and raising children. But all enslaved men, whether they lived with their families full time or just on weekends, had clearly defined notions of appropriate gendered behavior. Tending gardens or patches was a family enterprise led by men who expected to protect and provide for their families, while women's work fell into the realm of domestic duties. Custom and practice dictated enslaved wives should keep their cabins clean and tidy, cook and prepare food for their families, wash clothes, and raise their enslaved children to the best of their abilities in addition to laboring for their masters. But women only had a limited amount of time and energy to devote to household chores, sometimes facing the wrath of not only irate owners but also their husbands. Just as demanding as masters and mistresses when it came to matters domestic, husbands scolded them for neglecting their household duties. For example, when a South Carolina slave named Jim beat his wife, Maria, for not keeping their cabin tidy and clean, their mistress, Elizabeth Franklin Perry, was not sympathetic to Maria's plight. Instead, she blamed Maria for her own misfortune, accusing her of being an inferior housekeeper.

Physical domestic abuse certainly existed in slave society; however, surviving evidence about spousal violence—sexual or otherwise—is fairly scant. Slave women who published their autobiographies were more likely to describe white assaults. Some women recalled attempted sexual violence by black men in positions of power and authority, such as slave drivers, but very few mentioned such abuse at the hands of spouses. In the rare instances in which female respondents mentioned violent husbands, they tended to blame their owners for forcing or otherwise cajoling them into marriages with men they did not love. Rose Williams of Texas left her husband after emancipation because she had been forced by her master to marry him. Likewise, Lucy Skipwith used freedom's opportunities to leave her unsatisfactory marriage. In the post–Civil War era, some black women described beatings and attacks during slavery by male members of their households to Freedmen's Bureau officials, although this testimony was also fairly rare.

Marriage sometimes caused enslaved women considerable pain, grief, and unhappiness because living together as man and wife under a slave regime occasionally tipped spousal relationships into a state of conflict and discontent. Couples argued over the division of household chores, bickered over day-to-day activities, and occasionally tensions escalated to physical and sexual violence. Nonetheless, although female slaves were reluctant to divulge details of their personal relationships, evidence from the surviving testimony of enslaved women suggests that most spouses found their marriage provided a place of refuge, companionship, and support. Neither men nor women dominated enslaved families; they were neither patriarchal nor matriarchal. Instead, most enslaved families were characterized by a type of gender equality in which men and women worked together for a common good. Couples helped each other survive the brutality of their enslavement and its dehumanizing tendencies. Love and marriage provided enslaved women with a bulwark against oppression.

Marriages often led to children, but pregnancy granted enslaved women scant relief from field labor and served only to heighten the everyday burdens endured by women attempting to juggle their roles as workers and reproducers. Typically, owners granted enslaved women a maximum of one month's leave after they bore children, and the majority worked as well as they could until they felt the onset of labor. Some masters also gave pregnant enslaved women a degree of respite by moving them out of the fields and assigning lighter work such as spinning or carding. However, only a few allowed total rest for pregnancy-related illnesses or tiredness. These differing attitudes and policies indicate that most masters found themselves torn between regarding their enslaved women either primarily as workers or as reproducers.

Enslaved women mostly gave birth in their cabins. Usually only female slaves tended to them during childbirth. Millie Barber recalled, "I can't 'member us ever having a doctor on de place; just a granny was enough at childbirth." Ellen Godfrey similarly recalled, "Never have a doctor. Granny for me yet. My Mary good old granny. Catch two set o' twin for me."[7] Grannies were also healers; for example, Fred Forbes's mother was a "kind of a doctor" who made medicine for colds and sore throats. "Pussy" worked as a midwife, but she also ran the plantation hospital. Only on very large plantations did women give birth in plantation hospitals that had "lying in" wards. Most midwives learned their skills from their mothers, and they relied on a combination of practice, experience, and supernatural beliefs.

Occasionally slave women gave birth in the Big House, which allowed members of the slaveholding family to oversee the birth. Because owners had such a vested interest in achieving live births, they denied many enslaved women privacy during childbirth. Mistresses sometimes tried to direct doctors or enslaved midwives when their slave women gave birth, and many sought to be involved in labor and childbirth, even if only providing food and drink for new slave mothers. Pregnant enslaved women were sometimes forced subjects of medical experimentation by a new generation of gynecologists who were developing "scientific" procedures for childbirth. These men included J. Marion Sims, who coerced slave women suffering from tears to their vaginas, bladders, and bowels after childbirth to endure hours of agonizing operations, many of which were unsuccessful at repairing damage. Over the course of the nineteenth century, in part as a result of these experiments, childbirth became more of a medical procedure for both slaves and white women, and women had less of a say in how they delivered their babies. Mary Wooldridge worked as a midwife when enslaved in Kentucky. She lamented the loss of traditional grannies, and she considered modern-day medical practices as "tommy-rot." Mary's complaints exemplify some of the conflicts between "traditional" midwives and modern medical practitioners of the nineteenth century about best birthing practices.

Slave women also helped their white mistresses during and after childbirth. While owners expected the majority of enslaved women to return to work within no more than one month after childbirth, white mistresses had both the liberty and the practical help to spend longer periods of time confined to their beds. Female slaves assisted them and tended to their newborns. Some lactating slave women served as their mistresses' wet nurses, sharing their breast milk with white babies. Wet-nursing sapped the slave women's energies as well as their milk reserves, and some struggled to feed their own babies in addition to their mistress's white infants. Slave women often wet-nursed white babies because their mistresses had low milk supplies, but more often they performed this task to make their mistresses' lives less difficult. Mattie Logan recalled that her enslaved mother nursed all of their mistress's children because both women bore children at the same time.

Enslaved women's labor enabled owners to grow richer, but so did their reproductive capacities. Owners who prioritized their enslaved women's work rather than reproductive abilities forced mothers and infants apart. Nonetheless, masters, more concerned about the longer-term value of slave children, sometimes allowed women to carry suckling children on their backs as they labored. Others still permitted their female slaves to leave their babies and young children at the side of the fields while they worked. But the hot sun and threat of dangerous animals and insects caused much worry to enslaved women who sometimes preferred to leave their children in the care of other female slaves, either younger girls or older women, both of whom had limited value to their masters in the field. Separation from their beloved offspring made the time enslaved women spent with their children at the end of a working day all the more precious.

Female slaves were angry and frustrated that masters desired frequent childbearing for their own financial gain. These feelings turned to sheer terror when masters physically or sexually assaulted them. Examples of physical and sexual brutality survive in the testimony of enslaved and formerly enslaved women, but probing intimate issues can be difficult. Former slaves interviewed in the 1930s were often reluctant to discuss such personal and shameful matters with younger white interviewers, especially when questioned by men, and enslaved women who published autobiographies, including Harriet Jacobs, were famously discreet in their depictions of their sexual encounters with white men for fear of alienating their intended audience of white abolitionist women. Harriet Jacobs, enslaved in North Carolina, only obliquely described in her autobiography—under the pseudonym Linda Brent—how her master sexually harassed her while she labored as his domestic servant. Isolated and alone, Jacobs had no one to turn to for support, and the only response of her white mistress was a sense of ever-increasing jealousy toward Jacobs that manifested itself in violent anger. Along with the brutal physical punishments that enslaved women endured, sexual assault was a powerful means of enforcing control over female slaves because it instilled immense fear within them. Some enslaved women, like Harriet Jacobs, endured years of sexual assault from white men, from whom there was little hope of escape.

Physical punishment of slaves or rape of slave women was not a crime according to Southern state laws, a fact that effectively legitimized the physical and sexual abuse of enslaved women by whites. Slaves commonly endured whippings, but owners also beat, scratched, forced their female slaves into shackles, and rubbed salt or pepper into the open wounds they themselves inflicted. Some pregnant women had to dig holes in the ground for their stomachs to rest in to protect their valuable unborn children while masters whipped, paddled, or beat them. Nonetheless, some slaves fought against the abuse. The case of Celia, enslaved in Missouri, exemplifies slave women's vulnerability as well as their defiance. Purchased by Robert Newsom at age fourteen, Celia endured repeated rapes and bore him two children by the tender age of eighteen. After starting a relationship with another slave, Celia gained the strength to fight back and killed Newsom, a crime for which she was executed at age nineteen.

It is impossible to quantify the extent of sexual abuse enslaved women suffered. Not all victims bore mixed-race children because not all sexual encounters resulted in pregnancies. Moreover, slave women were reluctant to speak of their abuse, although a few revealed that they, or other female slaves, were involved in intimate relationships with whites, consensual or otherwise. Neither did white men commonly document their illicit sexual relationships with female slaves. South Carolina planter James Henry Hammond was rather atypical. He recorded in his diaries not only details of his relationship with his slave Sally Johnson, but also with her twelve-year-old daughter, Louisa. In a letter to his son, Harry, James Henry explained that he was not even sure which children were his own: "Sally says Henderson is my child. It is possible, but I do not believe it. . . . Louisa's first child *may* be mine. I think not. Her second I believe is mine." He went on to write, "Do not let Louisa or any of my children or possible children become slaves of strangers. Slavery *in the family* will be their happiest earthly condition."[8] Hammond saw his enslaved offspring purely as chattel, but at the same time, his faith in his own paternalism led him to believe that enslavement "within his family" was the best outcome for these children.

Not all intimate relationships between enslaved women and white men were the product of exploitation; some were based on mutual affection, despite the unequal status of the men and women involved. Enslaved women sometimes held long-standing relationships with white men, perhaps hoping their white lovers would provide them with material advantages such as better food and clothing, a decreased risk of sale and separation from their families, or even freedom itself. For example, Harriet Jacobs entered a sexual relationship with "Mr. Sands," a prominent white lawyer, in the hope of escaping the advances of her master, James Norcom. Jacobs hoped that Norcom might spurn her as a result of this relationship, or that her white lover might buy her, and even liberate her from enslavement. Indeed, there was a moment of personal triumph for Jacobs when she told Norcom that she was pregnant by another man. Thus Jacobs's relationships with white men illustrates the spectrum of these relationships, with forced sex at one end and voluntary, consensual involvement at the other.

In the antebellum era, Southern states became increasingly anxious about the number of white men entering sexual relationships with enslaved women, whom they subsequently freed, and they began increasingly to legislate against the manumission of enslaved women and their children. For example, in South Carolina white men had to petition state legislatures if they wanted to free slave women and children in their last wills and testaments, and by the 1850s all Southern states restricted manumissions in one way or another. Some states forbade the practice altogether by 1860, including Alabama, Arkansas, Florida, Georgia, Kentucky, Maryland, Mississippi, North Carolina, Tennessee, and Texas. Others, including Louisiana, South Carolina, and Virginia, all decreed that all manumitted slaves had to leave the state. Intimate relationships with white men also came at a cost for enslaved women who found themselves isolated—both physically and personally—from broader slave communities and lacked the support of their female peers. Moreover, some free black women expelled from their states upon manumission found themselves facing the undesirable prospect of having to leave their homes and families and starting a new life elsewhere. Freedom itself could therefore be problematic for slave and emancipated women.

White Southern women reacted to sexual liaisons between white men and enslaved women in a variety of ways. Some white women simply pretended they never occurred. Others responded with anger and jealousy toward the primary victims of their husbands' assaults. Overall, a shared womanhood did little to foster a sense of camaraderie between enslaved and white women. Mistresses could be just as brutal as men when it came to inflicting verbal and physical punishments, and slave women and girls who worked in the Big House were especially vulnerable to raising their mistresses' hackles. Cleaning, washing, cooking, and childcare all had to be performed to mistresses' often unreasonable expectations. Sex did not, therefore, unite slave and white women across racial lines in the antebellum South. But because white and enslaved women shared a gender, some female slaves approached their mistresses, rather than their masters, when in need of help or assistance. Regardless of mistresses' brutality, slave women often perceived their female owners as more compassionate than masters because both sets of women shared similar experiences as daughters, wives, and mothers. Enslaved women pleaded with their mistresses to use their influence with white masters; for example, in preventing slave sales or other forced separations.

Sometimes enslaved women sought mistresses' help or advice in the realms of health care and sickness, especially in matters related to reproduction because all women shared the same experience of monthly cycles, and most went through pregnancy and childbirth. Mistresses undoubtedly sympathized with their enslaved women who underwent difficult and sickly pregnancies and when they suffered miscarriages, endured long and painful labors, or lost their children at birth or thereafter. Women helped each other during pregnancy and childbirth and also shared customs and advice in matters of feeding, weaning, and nurturing infants. Some slave women appealed to their mistresses to avoid separating their families by sale or to treat the slaves more humanely. Yet enslavement ensured that close ties, even some friendships, were never based on equality because of white women's power over their slaves. The spectrum of relationships between enslaved and white women was complex and contradictory. While shared gender offered opportunities for some close ties, the sheer brutality and cruelty of some mistresses toward their female slaves ensured that friendships between the two remained elusive.

Plagued by their white masters and mistresses' hostility, callousness, and abuse, enslaved women retreated into a world of illicit resistance to bondage that was deeply influenced by their gender. Overt slave revolts were the domain of enslaved men, and running away was perilous even without having one's children in tow. While offspring inevitably brought great joy to mothers, they also tied women yet further to their quarters and restricted their ability to move. Childbearing capacities meant female slaves more commonly engaged in "day-to-day" forms of resistance such as the feigning of sickness and pregnancy rather than trying to overthrow the regime. Nonetheless, some women did run away. Sometimes married couples without children fled together. William and Ellen Craft escaped bondage prior to starting a family because they did not want to raise their children as slaves. Ellen Craft disguised herself as a white man, while William pretended to be her personal slave. It was rare for enslaved mothers to leave their children behind while they sought to flee bondage themselves. Harriet Jacobs escaped the clutches of her owner only because she was secure in the knowledge that her free grandmother would raise her children, Joseph and Louisa. Even so, before she escaped to the Northern states, Harriet hid for several years in her grandmother's small attic space where she could at least watch her children grow up while she remained free, if confined. However, Harriet Jacobs was unusual. Most enslaved women did not have free black grandmothers willing and able to raise their sons and daughters. Because slavery so often meant the involuntary separation of mothers and children, few women chose, like Harriet Jacobs, to separate themselves from their beloved offspring.

Some black women assisted others in their flight from enslavement. Following her own escape from bondage in 1849, Harriet Tubman returned to the South again and again to help other slaves, including some of her

Frontispiece image from William Craft, *Running a Thousand Miles for Freedom; Or, the Escape of William and Ellen Craft from Slavery* (London: William Tweedie, 1860). In *Documenting the American South*, The University of North Carolina at Chapel Hill. http://docsouth.unc.edu/neh/craft/frontis.html.

own extended family, flee to the North. Harriet worked for the so-called underground railroad, an informal network of escape routes, safe houses, and "conductors" who guided fugitive slaves across tricky terrain to the relative safety of the North.

Nonetheless, runaway slave advertisements suggest that between 1838 and 1860 women comprised just 19 percent of runaways, compared to 81 percent men. Tied to their children and frequently unfamiliar with neighboring terrain, it was certainly harder for women to escape slavery than it was for men, as Table 4.2 shows (p. 76).

Indeed, it was much easier for enslaved women to temporarily "truant" away from their quarters than flee bondage for good. Most of these female temporary runaways, like their male counterparts, simply sought a period of respite from the everyday toil of plantation labor, although sometimes women needed a break from more gendered forms of exploitation, including

Frontispiece image from Sarah H. Bradford, *Scenes in the Life of Harriet Tubman* (Auburn, NY: W. J. Moses Printer, 1869). Image of Harriet Tubman. In *Documenting the American South*, The University of North Carolina at Chapel Hill. http://docsouth.unc. edu/neh/bradford/frontis.html.

Table 4.2.   Gender of Runaways by State, Late Period, 1838–1860

	VA	NC	TN	SC	LA	Totals
Number of Females:	17	18	20	89	104	248
(percentage)	(9)	(14)	(12)	(19)	(29)	(19)
Number of Males:	178	114	148	369	259	1,068
(percentage)	(91)	(86)	(88)	(81)	(71)	(81)
Totals	**195**	**132**	**168**	**458**	**363**	**1,316**

Table from John Hope Franklin and Loren Schweninger, *Runaway Slaves: Rebels on the Plantation* (Oxford and New York: Oxford University Press, 1999), 212.

physical or sexual abuse. Sallie Smith remembered, rather poetically, how she sometimes ran so far from her plantation that she could no longer hear "the cows low or the roosters crow."[9] These fleeting moments of freedom gave Sallie Smith, and no doubt many other women, a precious sense of peace and tranquility away from the hustle, bustle, and violence of life in the quarters. Emmeline Heard's mother's escapes were more stressful, however. When whipped by her mistress she frequently ran away to the woods but had to sneak back home to her quarters every night to nurse her baby. Like so many other female slaves, motherhood tied Emmeline's mother to her quarters. Absenteeism therefore served a useful function for enslaved women unable or unwilling to try to escape permanently and reach the free states of the North. Women who truanted engaged in individual, rather than collective, resistance to the regime, albeit with a degree of community help; for example, when other women provided food or helped care for their children. But because absenteeism caused only temporary familial separations, it held much more appeal than permanent escape for enslaved women, who were less familiar with neighboring terrain than men.

Slave women also possessed a unique ability to effectively use their reproductive capacities to resist their enslavement in a number of ways. Some women attempted to control their own fertility. Occasionally, women wished not to bring enslaved infants into the world, not only because of the trials of bondage itself but also because they knew their children's economic value to their masters. In depriving slaveholders of new babies, enslaved women therefore limited whites' ability to generate profit from their offspring. Some enslaved women practiced abstinence as a means of avoiding children rather than using contraceptive techniques or abortifiacients. Sarah Shaw Graves claimed her enslaved mother married a sickly man precisely because she knew he could never father children. Other antebellum enslaved women, like their African ancestors, chewed cotton root in the belief it was an abortifiacient or contraceptive. Prolonged breast feeding, although not fail-safe, also diminished women's chances of becoming pregnant. William Byrd recalled that enslaved women chewed so they would not give birth. "All of their masters sho' did have to watch them, but sometimes they would slip out at night and get them a lot of cotton roots and bury them under their quarters."[10] Women's use of roots and herbs as possible abortifiacients created a sense of paranoia about their future profits among some slaveholders because they were powerless to prevent their slave women's various forms of "gynecological resistance."

The ability to reproduce was both a burden and an asset for female slaves, many of whom resisted enslavement though their reproductive abilities. Owners detected enslaved pregnancies through women's missed periods and growing stomachs. As a result, some female slaves feigned pregnancy in the hope of receiving a lighter workload or some temporary respite from arduous field labor from their masters. Virginian planter Landon Carter described how his slave, Sarah, claimed to be expecting for eleven months prior to giving birth. Upon Sarah's next pregnancy, Carter confronted her. But Sarah then ran off to the woods for over a week despite being "big with child." Sarah's two popular forms of "day-to-day" resistance were well-suited to female slaves. She denied Carter the value of her labor through truanting and presented him with a dilemma over whether to regard her primarily as a worker or a reproducer. Enslaved women felt empowered when they denied their owners the value of their labor and grasped whatever opportunities they could to gain a measure of relief from slavery. Masters' regard for their female chattels' reproductive abilities meant they tended to give women the benefit of the doubt in matters related to their pregnancies, and this represented a small, but significant, victory for enslaved women in their everyday battles with owners.

Using their reproductive capacities as one form of resistance, enslaved women did what they could to protest their status. Like enslaved men, female slaves also partook in more general acts of defiance, including feigning sickness or clumsiness; damaging tools, livestock, or crops; or practicing self-mutilation to decrease their value. Occasionally, enslaved women lashed out against their owners. Clorry belonged to Edward Fuller, president of the First National Bank of Charleston, South Carolina. When Mrs. Fuller criticized Clorry's washing, Clorry lashed out violently, causing Mrs. Fuller, who was pregnant, to give birth. Clorry was then severely whipped—by whom remains unknown, nor does any evidence survive about whether Mrs. Fuller's baby lived or died. These individual acts of rebellion did not threaten the regime as a whole, but it gave slave women a small sense of satisfaction, even when they knew their owners would punish them. By neither internalizing nor accepting their bondage, female slaves gained a small but significant sense of power.

Antebellum enslaved women's status and prestige among their peers, if not their owners, grew over the course of their lives, and mature women steered those younger than themselves in a moral direction while at the same time recognizing the necessity of rather more pragmatic approaches to life at times. In general, flexibility, adaptability, pragmatism, strength, and resilience characterized the lives of female slaves, and they tried to pass on these character traits to their children. Slave mothers tried to raise their offspring with an understanding of how to negotiate their slave status, just as their own mothers had done for them. They warned their children about appropriate modes of behavior in front of whites and instilled in their daughters a sense of the dangers posed by white sexual assault. Such survival tactics taught children valuable lessons about how to survive slavery as an adult. Slave women taught children from a very young age about status differences between blacks and whites; for example, that the children of their owners must be addressed as "young master" or "young mistress." At other times, female slaves told stories or sang songs to their children with melancholy lyrics that depicted the horrors of physical punishments, sale, and separation. But despite their best efforts, all parents failed to shield their children from the burden of bondage itself.

Although slave women spent much of their time laboring for whites, in the precious hours they spent with their families and broader communities, enslaved girls and women turned to other female slaves—to their mothers, sisters, grandmothers, aunts, cousins, and friends—for support and advice about strategies for surviving slavery. Elderly women were especially revered for their experience and knowledge and, notwithstanding the devastating effects of sales and separations, slave women often had many strong and powerful senior female role models. Grandmothers were especially revered as educators of younger women, advising them how to survive and resist their enslavement. For example, Molly Horniblow had an extremely close relationship with her granddaughter, Harriet Jacobs, especially following the death of Harriet's mother when she was just six years old. Harriet credited her remarkable grandmother for the "many comforts" she provided. Molly even attempted to purchase her granddaughter from her owner when she suspected that he was sexually abusing Harriet. However, the owner denied her frequent requests. Senior and respected women like Molly also took responsibility for the moral upbringing of slave girls. When Harriet became pregnant by her white lover—hoping he would buy and release her—Molly reacted furiously, telling Harriet she was a disgrace to her dead mother.

The private and personal worlds of enslaved women within broader enslaved communities were complex. Female slaves battled with their owners over their family formations, their weddings and their marriages, and their relationships with their children, whom women fought hard to raise according to their own values, not those of their white owners. But because they were the legal property of their masters, enslaved women had no legal rights over their children, or, indeed, their own bodies. Motherhood therefore represented a double-edged sword for enslaved women. Although they loved their children dearly, offspring increased the workload of mothers who had to care for children as well as labor for their masters. Mothers also worried about their children's future as slaves, especially their daughters. Moreover, enslaved women resented their masters for making profits from their beloved offspring and for not giving mothers enough time off work to adequately care for their children.

Gender-specific ordeals gave enslaved women a sense of camaraderie about their enslavement, and how, practically, they had to negotiate their oppression and formulate tactics of resistance via peer support networks. More tied to their quarters than enslaved men, many female slaves lived in a narrow, bleak world. But because gender mattered to enslaved women, they shared with each other networks of support that depended upon female relatives—both immediate and more distant—as well as female friendships. Furthermore, enslaved women relied upon each other not simply because the brutality of slavery meant that they *had* to depend on one other but because their shared experiences meant they *wanted* to help each other. Antebellum enslaved women enjoyed the safety and security of their own well-established gender networks, and their families and friendships brought women feelings of hope and joy, glimpses of optimism within the wider context of slavery's oppression.

Notes

1. Gus Feaster in George P. Rawick, *The American Slave, South Carolina Narratives, Vol. 2, Part 2* (Westport, CT: Greenwood Press, 1972), 65–66.

2. Letter to Benjamin Franklin Perry from Elizabeth Perry, "Monday afternoon," [no year], Benjamin Franklin Perry Papers, South Caroliniana Library, University of South Carolina.

3. George Fleming in George P. Rawick, *The American Slave: Supplement Series 1, North Carolina and South Carolina Narratives, Vol. 11* (Westport, CT: Greenwood Press, 1977), 127–8.

4. Susan Hamlin in Rawick, *The American Slave, South Carolina Narratives, Vol. 2, Part 2*, 231–2.

5. Harriet Jacobs, *Incidents in the Life of a Slave Girl* (Boston, 1860).

6. Letter to Mr. J. F. Cooper [overseer at Gowrie plantation] from Charles Manigault, January 10, 1848, Letterbook 1846–48, Charles Izard Manigault Papers, South Caroliniana Library.

7. Millie Barber in Rawick, *The American Slave, South Carolina Narratives, Vol. 2, Part 1*, 39; Ellen Godfrey in Rawick, *The American Slave, South Carolina Narratives, Vol. 2, Part 2*, 62.

8. See Carol Bleser (ed.), *Secret and Sacred: The Diaries of James Henry Hammond, a Southern Slaveholder* (New York and Oxford: Oxford University Press, 1988), 18–19.

9. Quoted in Stephanie Camp, *Closer to Freedom: Enslaved Women and Everyday Resistance in the Plantation South* (Chapel Hill and London: University of North Carolina Press, 2004), 40.

10. William Byrd in the WPA narratives online: *Supplement Series 2, Texas Narratives, Vol. 3, Part 2*, 568. Library of Congress, http://memory.loc.gov/ammem/snhtml/snhome.html.

CHAPTER FIVE

~

Enslaved Women in the Civil War

The bloody battle between the North and the South of 1861 to 1865 altered the lives of all Americans, enslaved or otherwise, but it affected slave men and women in different ways. The conflict enabled some enslaved women to change their lives for the better, while others found the unique hardships of war almost impossible to bear. The Civil War also changed the nature of relationships between enslaved women and their white counterparts. Confederate conscription laws drafted white men into the military beginning in 1862, thus leaving white women to run plantations, farms, and homes. Denied the traditional support of husbands, fathers, and other male kin, enslaved women had to stoically bear the burden of wartime disruption alone. Like white women, female slaves missed their men, worrying about them on a daily basis, and news of injury or death caused women great heartbreak and anguish. Many white women vented their anger upon their female slaves, but both black and white women had to find new and innovative ways to run their households. Some enslaved women continued to live out their everyday lives to the same rhythms as they always had, regardless of the political and military turmoil striking at the heart of the United States. The fight between Blue and Gray was, for black women, often overshadowed by more immediate concerns about their everyday survival, protecting children, and staving off poverty, hunger, and ill health. But the war also increased women's gendered and racial oppression in the form of physical and sexual assaults by soldiers and by the economic hardships it caused.

As they had during the American Revolution, slave women mostly fought their battles for freedom at home. Sometimes they merely gained a newfound confidence to answer back to their mistresses. But other black women fought more directly for their freedom by running away, supporting the Union army, or seeking freedom in a personal as well as a general sense. Some slave women found opportunities for economic independence from white owners or from black men, while others saw the upheaval and chaos created by the war as a chance to search for beloved family members from whom they had been forcibly separated. Moreover, war created opportunities for women to move around and off the plantation, and this mobility did much to undermine the stability of slavery.

The arrival of war led to increased separations of enslaved men and women. The Confederate army forced male slaves into service, firstly at state level, and then through the Confederate Impressment Law of March 1863. Enslaved women grew anxious about their men leaving home, forced into fighting for the continuation of bondage. Like their white counterparts, enslaved women worried that their husbands and sons might never return home while they were left with additional work. Enslaved women had always performed the bulk of domestic work within their homes prior to the Civil War, but their men played important supporting roles, and women missed men's emotional support and practical help. During slavery, fathers and husbands assisted women in raising children. They had tended to gardens where families grew produce and raised livestock. These goods provided important supplementary food to be either eaten or bartered for other much-needed provisions. Men had also hunted and fished to support their families.

However, when the Confederacy forced them to serve in the army, enslaved women and children were denied these important supplementary foods, putting them at greater risk of malnutrition and ill health. The Civil War sometimes meant permanent separation from slave husbands with whom black women had previously lived in abroad marriages. In antebellum times, these unions worked because, providing the distances involved were not too great, husbands made great efforts to visit wives and children on weekends. But during the conflict, many masters made the decision to move themselves and their slaves to areas they deemed "safer." Former slave Harriet Robinson recalled that her white owners, fearing the arrival of Union troops, moved everyone on the plantation to a "safe place." In such distant accommodations, enslaved women could not turn to their abroad husbands for support, intimacy, and companionship.

As both black and white men departed in increasingly large numbers to the battle lines, ever greater demands were placed on enslaved women's labor. Women continued laboring on their farms and plantations in the same way as they always had. Field women hoed, seed, weeded, and picked in the often harsh, hot climate of the Southern states. But black women who had previously spent their time working within their owners' Big Houses now found that cooking, cleaning, polishing, washing, and tending to their mistresses' everyday whims were no longer a priority. Instead, female house servants had to join those who worked in the fields. Expected to perform labor traditionally reserved for enslaved men, including plowing, heaving, lifting, and mending fences and other equipment, women's work grew even more backbreaking.

The Civil War, like other conflicts, challenged accepted gendered conventions about labor for all women. For example, ex-slave Alice Sewell remembered how on her Alabama plantation all slaves stopped growing cotton during the war, and instead grew food for Confederate soldiers. Aged just thirteen when the conflict erupted, she also recalled packing up cotton in bales ready for storage, a task previously performed by enslaved men. Regardless of their tasks prior to the war, enslaved women, both young and old, did more arduous physical labor outdoors between 1861 and 1865. Some felt a sense of pride in their accomplishments, which proved women's physical capabilities and strength even as they lamented their aching muscles at the end of a strenuous day in the sun. But at the same time, the conflict sapped female slaves of their much-needed energies. They had their own cabins to run and children to care for, and the stresses of war imposed greater demands on their precious time. Some former house slaves also regarded field labor as somehow "defeminizing." And for women such as Alice Sewell, being forced to grow food for Confederate soldiers was a bitter pill to swallow. These men were fighting for the continuation of slavery and consuming scarce food. During wartime, enslaved women were expected to survive, to feed themselves and their children on ever more scant rations since whites deemed them to be the "least important" people to feed.

Hiring out enslaved women also grew more common during the Civil War because the practice provided slaveholders with much-needed cash. Most hired-out female slaves worked as servants, cooks, and laundresses to Confederate soldiers, sometimes working at temporary field hospitals or other military quarters. Although this type of work was physically easier and more rewarding than field labor, it often came at great personal cost because being hired out to Confederates meant that enslaved women were separated from their family members. Enslaved women also bitterly resented being forced into yet more domestic labor for white people who were fighting to defend slavery.

The practice of hiring out enslaved women within cities, already fairly commonplace, increased during the conflict. Overall, the institution of bondage necessarily became more flexible as the circumstances of war made it hard to engage in any long-term planning. Thus, hiring out slave women on a daily basis became more common, rather than entering into the monthly or yearly contracts that had been typical during the antebellum era. Ellen Campbell recalled her mistress taking her during the war to Augusta, Georgia, where Ellen was subsequently "rented" out daily to help a white woman with domestic chores at her boarding house. Thrown into an increasingly female environment during the Civil War, Ellen Campbell was not alone. War tended to separate men from women, husbands from wives, and mothers from male offspring.

Moreover, because enslaved women rated below white men, white women, free people of color, and slave men in terms of social status, female slaves bore the brunt of wartime shortages. Union blockades meant short supplies of everyday provisions and prevented Southerners from selling their goods and produce elsewhere, rendering money scarce. Food supplies grew scant, more mundane, and ever more expensive. Enslaved women became increasingly unsettled, their unease about the future made worse by the gnawing hunger in their stomachs. Women worried they would not have enough to eat, especially because mothers prioritized their children's nutrition above their own. Hunger among both female slaves and their offspring rose. Inadequate nutrition also made it hard for enslaved mothers to nurse their babies because they were unable to produce enough milk to feed them. The war heightened infant mortality rates, and women and children became more prone to sickness and disease. In 1862, a smallpox epidemic began in Washington, D.C., and then spread to the Upper South in 1863 to 1864 and to the Lower South and Mississippi Valley in 1865. The virus hit both Union and Confederate forces, both freedpeople and slaves alike. Other black women were affected by yellow fever, cholera, dysentery, and malnutrition. Already frail and sickly enslaved women were particularly susceptible to disease and death, or bore witness to their children's illnesses and passing.

Although spared the dangers of the battlefields, many enslaved women were the primary victims of economic hardship as Southern plantations and farms tightened their belts in wartime. For example, South Carolina slaveholder Thomas Porcher Ravenel, in his early efforts at wartime economizing, decreed that while his enslaved men still needed pants, his less important bondwomen could do without. Ravenel regarded his female slaves as less important because their physical labor did not match that of his enslaved men. During the Civil War, slaveholders as a whole became less concerned with the reproduction of their slave labor force and more worried about simply surviving the conflict. Whereas before the war, enslaved women's reproductive capacities gave them value, in wartime masters increasingly viewed their bondwomen as less capable workers, if not an outright burden. Owners fed them less and expected them to do more. Enslaved women themselves consequently grew more and more exhausted, more concerned about the future, and ever more hungry, all of which had a negative impact on their physical and mental well-being.

The war not only affected enslaved women's working and living conditions, it also fundamentally changed female slaves' relationships with white people. Left behind on the plantations and farms of white owners, many enslaved women were demoralized. On a day-to-day basis women had to resist physical and sexual assaults as well as masters' and mistresses' efforts to coerce them into ever harder physical labor. White masters knew that their slave regime was threatened in part by slaves fighting for the Union cause. When enslaved men joined the Union troops, leaving behind their spouses and children, some owners inflicted brutal repercussions on the female slaves left behind. A journalist for the *Boston Traveller* reported seeing black women being whipped and abused by their white masters in New Orleans because their sons, husbands, and fathers had enlisted with the Union forces. Frances Wilson filed a lengthy report to authorities in a Union camp in Kentucky in which she described her mistreatment at the hands of her master following her husband's enlistment in the Union army.

Not surprisingly, some enslaved women rejoiced when their white masters left to fight on the battlefields, or fled their homes in a state of fear and apprehension because they hoped to be left in peace, in a world without physical or sexual violence. These black women bore the brunt of white wrath because of their husbands' actions, but many former slave women spoke with great pride about their husbands' efforts on behalf of the Union army. Candis Goodwin proudly recalled that her husband, Jake, was a Union soldier: "He big man in dey war. He drill soldiers e'vy day. . . . He wucked up to be sergeant-major, in de Tenth regiment. Jacob Goodwin his name was. He say all look up to him an' 'spect him too."[1]

Enslaved women's relationships with their white mistresses also grew more volatile as masters departed for the battlefields, leaving black and white women thrown together in close proximity. White women became increasingly consumed by anger, bitterness, and hatred toward their bondwomen as they struggled to cope with the day-to-day management of their plantations and slave labor force, with which many had very little prior experience. During the antebellum era, white mistresses had often managed to convince themselves that their slave women were utterly devoted to them and would never leave. The Civil War, however, proved white women's perceptions of benign bondage to be very much at odds with reality. Female slaves grew ever more confident in protesting their status, wanting to labor for themselves and their families rather than serve white women. Thus, tensions grew between black and white women trying to fend for themselves and their children in an ever more uncertain and violent world.

White women resented having to reach out to their enslaved women for help, explanation, and assistance because this exposed their vulnerability in the absence of men. The trials of war also affected aristocratic white women's sense of their own femininity as they began, some for the first time, to do manual labor, performing tasks traditionally reserved for men or enslaved women. Furthermore, the longer the war continued, the more types of work black and white women had to do. Some husbands, fathers, and sons never returned from battle. And as emancipation became a very real possibility, white women were forced, sometimes for the very first time, to imagine their future without relying on slaves to perform all their chores. For some, such a future was beyond comprehension. Amelia Lines wrote in 1862 that without her domestic slaves she could not look nice or keep her baby or house clean. She failed to recognize her female slaves as fellow women who also wanted to look nice and have clean babies and homes. Although the conflict imposed some similar hardships on slave and white women's lives, the two groups grew ever more divided by their race as the conflict raged on.

The Civil War threw simmering tensions between enslaved and white women into sharp focus. Unlike enslaved women, for whom friendships with their fellow female slaves remained paramount during the war, white women struggled to find the time for neighborly friendships and the support of their peers. Mistresses worried, too, about their prior treatment of their female slaves now that they had no male "protection." Might their enslaved women seek revenge for past cruelty they inflicted? White women detected changes in their slaves' attitudes as the scent of freedom grew stronger. In turn, enslaved women's confidence blossomed as they relished their ability to talk back or challenge their mistresses' decisions, or simply refused to perform the labor white women assigned to them. Mattie J. Jackson and her mother, enslaved in Missouri, took great delight in hearing news of Union progress, and they made no attempt to hide their pleasure from their white mistress, much to her chagrin.

Other female slaves left their quarters to visit kin without their mistresses' consent, and regardless of the material hardships imposed by war, black women began to live fuller, more mobile lives. Thus, in some ways, the war brought positive changes to enslaved women's lives. A few mistresses even began to question the slave regime and their role within it in their private correspondence and journals. However, testimony from Union soldiers also describes white women's inhumane treatment of female slaves. As white women's stress levels rose, they were more likely to subject their female slaves to physical or verbal abuse. In Augusta, Georgia, Ellen Campbell endured a brutal attack by the white female owner of the boarding house to whom she was hired out. Luckily, Ellen's horrified mistress revoked the contract and allowed her slave to return home. But as the Union army advanced into the South, more and more enslaved women found themselves engaged in their own, intimate war with their white mistresses.

As whites abandoned their homes in fear or left to fight, a great many enslaved women were left to run abandoned plantations and farms themselves. Former slave Annie L. Burton noted the irony of witnessing white people running from their homes just as slaves themselves had done many years previously. Her own master fled their plantation in Alabama, hoping to bury his possessions, but Union troops caught him and confiscated all his goods. Curious female slaves left alone on farms and plantations had no qualms about exploring the private worlds their masters and mistresses had left behind, a side of plantation life to which they had traditionally been denied access. Some women ventured into their mistresses' bedrooms and dressing chambers to try on, and sometimes take, the white women's clothes and jewelry. Some women chose highly impractical items. In the excitable climate of emancipation, they took frivolous possessions such as lace, ribbons, and trinkets. Stealing such personal and valued items from their mistresses gave female slaves a strong sense of empowerment, and it granted them opportunities for expressing their own femininity. Mocking and mimicking the white women who held them in bondage provided a chance for slave women to have fun while rejecting their enslaved status.

Even as they lived in a world largely dominated by women, enslaved women continued to experience sexual assaults by men. Rape was an inevitable consequence of war, especially the new, "total" war of General Sherman's forces as they wreaked havoc on their infamous march. Armies shot, stole, attacked, raped, and destroyed property. They razed to the ground plantation mansions and slave cabins alike, regardless of attempts by blacks and whites to defend themselves and their property. Negative stereotypes of black women—whether free or enslaved—as promiscuous "Jezebel" figures also contributed to the notion that they actively invited sexual advances from white men. Indeed, the war increased the pool of potential abusers. Black women's aggressors included Confederate and Union soldiers, their masters, or other white men, as well as black men. Black women thus bore the burden of sexual assaults before, during, and after the conflict.

Former slave Tena White, though rather guarded about her experiences, recalled: "My mother raise me right. When de Yankee come through we been at Remley Point. My ma took care ob me. She shut me up and she guard me. De Yankee been go in de colored people house, an dey mix all up, and dey do jus what dey want. Dey been brutish." Eliza Hasty was slightly more open, remembering that "de Yankees come. They took notice of me! They was a bad lot dat disgrace Mr. Lincoln dat sent them here. They insult women both white and black, but de Lord was mindful of his own." Bessie Lawson explained that soldiers "stole" her mother during the war, forcing her to remain in their camp. When she returned, "She had a white chile."[2] Nonetheless, the Union and Confederate armies did not condone the rape of civilians, including slaves. In 1863, six white officers stationed in Fort Jackson, Louisiana, were dismissed from the U.S. Army for attempting to rape African American laundresses in their command. Moreover, despite many atrocities, the departure of white men to fight for the Confederate cause liberated some enslaved women from sexual abuse. Some black women who remained at home could relax a little more, worry less, enjoy their families, and take pride in their homes despite the arduous nature of their day-to-day wartime labor.

Not all slave women remained on the plantations and farms of their white owners. Isolation, as well as other forms of wartime adversity and violence, led some enslaved women to make the momentous decision to run away. However, only the bravest or most desperate women sought to flee. Prior to the war, enslaved women found escape particularly difficult because only a small minority performed roles that routinely took them away from their quarters, and masters usually only issued passes to men to visit nearby spouses and children. Whites who encountered enslaved women away from their plantations were suspicious, and escapees had to contend with patrollers and their bloodthirsty dogs as well as the sheer physical difficulty of negotiating the Southern terrain. But because the conflict upset traditional notions of gender-appropriate behavior, it became more common to see enslaved women away from their quarters, especially since most white men could no longer supervise their slaves' mobility. Some slave women used these new opportunities to visit family members living elsewhere, particularly their "abroad" husbands. Other women, though, were bolder, making the decision to flee slavery. Women fled alone, or sometimes with their children because they could not bear the thought of leaving them behind. Some who fled tried to find missing husbands, parents, children, and other beloved kin, while others sought Union lines in the hope of playing a role in ending slavery.

Others still hoped to reach the safety of the Northern states where freedom beckoned. Some women simply could no longer tolerate verbal, physical, or sexual abuse at the hands of white women or men and hastily fled without any thought about where they might go.

Some left to work for the Union cause. Female runaways sometimes hoped to reach Union lines, while others, by virtue of their location, found themselves supporting Union troops relatively early on in the conflict. For example, Union forces gained control of South Carolina's Port Royal Sound in late 1861. In response, black men and women flocked to the area either seeking Union help or hoping to play a role in defeating the Confederacy. Indeed, throughout the South, Union forces increasingly recognized the value of enslaved labor. Men performed a variety of camp labor, usually without receiving pay. Some, such as those in Port Royal, received a small military wage, but it was rarely sufficient for them to support their families. Military authorities could not decide on the roles of enslaved women within Union camps. By May 1863 there were around twenty-three thousand slaves inside Union lines in occupied parts of Virginia, 45 percent of whom were female.

Based on a white, middle-class notion that women were always dependent on men, Union officials defined these women only as *wives*, rather than granting them supplies or wages as individuals in their own right. Union troops usually provided only the black men with paid work, expecting them to provide for their families. Such attitudes displayed inherent ironies. Prior to their escape, enslaved women had lived in a variety of different family forms. Few slave women depended financially upon their men for support, and some arrived in Union camps alone. Even if the very concept of financial dependency had been familiar to them, the black women in the camps simply could not financially depend upon poorly paid men. Some military officials attempted to tax black men's wages to raise funds for the support of their dependents, but these attempts failed because black men earned so little.

Union authorities rather naively saw legal marriage as a solution to the "problem" of feeding, clothing, and housing contraband slaves. Wedlock, they believed, rendered black women dependent upon *husbands*, not Union troops and their much-needed rations. Aside from economic motivations, the Union army was keen to enforce legal marriage among black people because, believing in racist stereotypes of blacks as immoral and promiscuous, officials thought it would encourage stable families. In maintaining such stereotypes, whites conveniently ignored prior efforts by the enslaved, whether or not their marriages had legal sanction, to maintain their families despite frequent forced sales and separations. Some women questioned why such legitimization was necessary. Enslaved couples had undergone wedding ceremonies and celebrations sometimes sanctioned by their white owners, and many formerly enslaved women regarded their marriage unions as already legal in the eyes of God. But enslaved wedlock had not been legally valid, so for some women, legitimizing their matrimony under American law was very important. Former slave Hannah Guy remembered that a regimental chaplain lined up her and her husband, Henry, as well as other refugees, and married them all collectively by reading out a list of their names. She valued the legitimization of her marriage, despite her disappointment about the lack of pomp and ceremony. Military authorities may have used marriage as an attempt to control and manage black women. Nonetheless, while opinions among black women varied, there is no doubt that formalizing their marriages before a Union clergyman was ultimately a romantic gesture between black men and women. Thus in some ways, the ability to legally marry the men they loved was also a clear sign of women's freedom.

For black women, life behind Union lines was often a disappointment. The struggle for everyday survival was no easier, and sometimes even harder, than under slavery. Although most black women believed that they would be "perfectly safe" in joining the Union forces, the reality of camp life did not match expectations. Although she was only a child during the war itself, Annie L. Burton remembered how "the Yankee soldiers found that they had such an army of men, women and children that they had to build tents and feed them to keep them from starving. But from what I, a little child, saw and heard the older ones say, that must have been a terrible time of trouble."[3] Many Union forces simply did not want to take on female former slaves. Their army needed soldiers, fighters, and strong field workers, and Union troops considered enslaved women as unsuitable for all of these tasks, despite their years of backbreaking labor as slaves and the legacy of black women's hard outdoor labor during bondage. Instead, Union authorities defined black women as burdens rather than as strong and valuable assets.

Part of the problem was that Union forces lacked an overall policy to deal with the vast numbers of black people seeking their support. The Union army had only scant resources, and regiments struggled to provide for the soldiers, let alone the black men, women, and children who flocked to the Union lines in search of help. Should they accept slaves as free people or as "contraband" property? In 1861 and 1862, Congress passed two Confiscation Acts that allowed the military to confiscate all slaves who served in the Confederate military as well as those belonging to disloyal Southerners in areas occupied by Union forces. If their owners did not surrender within sixty days, the courts could free those slaves. However, these acts were not uniformly enforced. In areas such as the Mississippi Valley and the border states, troops sometimes excluded all fugitive slaves from their camps. Some military officials, refusing to take any responsibility for the families of the black soldiers who had enlisted, simply evicted black women and children from camps.

Expulsion could have dire consequences. Joseph Miller, after fleeing slavery, served with the 124th U.S. Colored Infantry. Based in a Kentucky camp with his wife and four children, Miller's account of camp life is testament to the horrific conditions black families faced once they entered Union lines. The authorities forced Miller's wife and children to leave the camp despite the fact that they were ill. Their son subsequently died, causing yet more anguish for the family. Julia Wilbur, an agent of the Rochester Ladies Anti-Slavery Society, found other former slaves in Alexandria, Virginia, held in prison because there was nowhere else for them to go. Wilbur described women and children, many of whom were extremely sick and cold, lying in damp areas without any bedding. Not surprisingly, women and children were especially vulnerable to the outbreaks of smallpox and other diseases that swept the South throughout the war.

Undoubtedly shocked by the Union forces' lack of support, many black women had no alternative but to return to the plantations and farms of their former owners to continue to eke out a day-to-day existence. Other masters cajoled or persuaded their enslaved women to return to the plantations. Mattie J. Jackson lived in a Union camp for three weeks before her owner, Mr. Lewis, tricked her into returning home. Lewis told Mattie that her mother was "anxious" for her to return, so Mattie reluctantly agreed to leave the camp. However, instead of taking her home to her mother, Lewis punished Mattie Jackson for seeking refuge with the Union troops by putting her up for sale in a trader's yard.

Those enslaved women who stayed in the camps tried to maintain their independence and freedom. They relied on their enterprising spirits, and they raised funds to feed themselves and their families by selling or bartering goods they had produced. Like Southern slaveholders before them, Union officials stereotyped black women, imagining them only in roles they had held in slavery as field workers, cooks, and laundresses. In January 1864, for example, the U.S. War Department issued an order permitting all general hospitals under U.S. jurisdiction to hire African American women as cooks or nurses. When possible, black women rejected the "formal" labor offered to them in Union camps because this type of work reminded them of slave labor. Black women in Union camps often declined paid labor, preferring to support their families without depending on white people. They wanted to be able to work at their own pace and fit their labor around their families' needs. Nonetheless, more practical concerns for everyday survival led some black women to take advantages of the opportunities Union troops provided, if on their own terms. Ellen Campbell recalled black women traveling to a Union camp next to a river near her home in Augusta to wash troops' clothes "fer a good price."[4] Susie King Taylor, who ran away from her quarters in Georgia aged just thirteen to join other "contraband" slaves in the Union-occupied coastal areas, worked as a laundress for Union forces on St. Simon's Island. Women also continued to draw on mutual support networks to help each other in the camps just as they had done during their enslavement.

Frontispiece image from Susie King Taylor, *Reminiscences of My Life in Camp with the 33rd United States Colored Troops Late 1st S.C. Volunteers* (Boston: The Author, 1902). In *Documenting the American South*, The University of North Carolina at Chapel Hill, http://docsouth.unc.edu/neh/taylorsu/frontis.html.

But the numbers of people in the camps kept increasing. Abraham Lincoln was well aware that Confederate forces relied upon enslaved labor for support and provisions. In the fall of 1862, primarily as a military tactic, the president warned the Confederacy that if they did not stop their insurrection by the end of the year, he would issue a proclamation freeing any slave in a state that was still in rebellion. Since none of the rebel states heeded his warning, on January 1, 1863, he signed the Emancipation Proclamation, freeing all slaves in the Confederate states. As the proclamation only freed slaves in states that had seceded from the United States, where the Union had little hope of enforcing it, it was clearly more propaganda than substance. But Lincoln's Proclamation inevitably encouraged more slave men to leave for the Union army to provide additional manpower as, indeed, Lincoln and his advisors had hoped. How formerly enslaved women might respond was not at the forefront of these men's minds.

Following the Emancipation Proclamation, fugitive slaves also joined black men and women in Union-occupied areas. Defined as "contrabands of war," black fugitives were not legally free. Indeed, the status of these refugees was unclear, since the proclamation applied only to slaves in the Confederacy. In April 1863, an enslaved woman named Dolly ran away from Louis Manigault's Charleston home where she had worked as a domestic. Dolly's master asked the Charleston police for help retrieving her. He designed a poster that included a picture of Dolly and offered "fifty dollars reward" for her return (p. 94). Manigault believed a white man had "enticed" his slave to escape, and while Dolly left no evidence about her motives, it is certainly possible she took advantage of wartime disruption and uncertainty by fleeing Manigault's oppressive household.

Enslaved women grasped the opportunities war provided with both hands. They ran away in the hope of reuniting with family members, seeking those wrenched away from them through the domestic slave trade or by planters who had migrated west. Indeed, female slaves' first taste of emancipation was bound up with the liberty to move freely. Union authorities also realized that this movement was useful for their own military purposes. But as the numbers of refugees rose, black women and children became increasingly confined within overcrowded and unsanitary camps, lacking adequate food, clothing, and shelter. Life in the camps was often not materially any better than life had been on white owners' plantations and farms. Sometimes Union soldiers stole livestock or other produce from black families. Removed from their extended support networks, women in camps argued with their spouses and with each other as all faced an uncertain future defined largely by poverty.

When Received.	Coveyance.	No. of bush. Rough Rice.	No. of bbls. Clean Rice.	No. of bus. to the bbl.	Price.	Date of Sales.	Gross Amount of Sales.	Nett Amount of Sales.

$ 50.00 Reward !!

Ran away from the Yard Corner of Jackson & Broad Streets, Augusta Ga. — on the evening of Tuesday 7th April 1863 a Woman "Dolly", whose likeness is here seen! —
She is thirty years of age, light complexion — hesitates somewhat when spoken to, and is not a very healthy woman — but rather good looking, with a fine set of teeth. Never changed her Owner and has been a house Servant always. — It is thought she has been enticed off by some White Man, being herself a Stranger to this City, and belonging to a Charleston family. —
For further particulars apply to Antoine Poullain Esq — Augusta Ga. —

Augusta Police Station
Louis Manigault, Owner of Dolly

Original image held in the Manigault Family Papers, Southern Historical Collection, Manuscripts Collection, Wilson Library, University of North Carolina, Chapel Hill.

The Emancipation Proclamation of 1863 did not have an immediate impact upon enslaved women, many of whom continued with their day-to-day lives and labors just as they always had. Some callous masters attempted to keep news of the proclamation a secret. But news of emancipation seems instead to have slowly and steadily sunk in. Some black women left the plantations where they had lived as slaves to seek Union-occupied areas. Yet others remained awaiting the return of family members. Nonetheless, they all contemplated their new lives as freewomen. When, in 1865, the Thirteenth Amendment finally abolished slavery in the United States, slave women were overjoyed. They sang, danced, and thanked God that their time in bondage was over. A carnival atmosphere prevailed. But after this initial euphoria, enslaved women began to question their future. Some former owners insisted that all freedpeople leave their plantations and farms as soon as possible because they could no longer "support" them. Other former masters hid news about emancipation for as long as possible and thereafter continued to expect freedpeople to work for them just as they had during slavery. Following emancipation, freedwomen worried about economic and social concerns rather than their legal status. Women wondered how to provide for themselves and their families, and how they might reunite with those from whom they had been forcibly separated. Some freedwomen went searching across the South for their loved ones. Annie L. Burton's mother had previously run away from her Alabama plantation after a whipping, leaving her three children behind. Following the end of slavery, she returned to collect her offspring only to find that her mistress refused to relinquish the three children. She had to return under the cover of darkness to "steal" her own free children. Emancipation was a piecemeal, gradual process rather than one celebratory day of jubilee.

Overall, the Civil War provided black women with an ever-increasing variety of experiences. On plantations, farms, and urban areas, women might live under Union or Confederate rule. But white men, whether they were Southern slaveholders or Union troops, forced black women to work ever harder and for longer hours. When it suited them, they forced black women to perform tasks traditionally reserved for men, and they cut women's rations and clothing supplies, affecting not just black women themselves but also their offspring. Some women found their lives changed for the better. As they took on more roles traditionally reserved for men, some had more opportunities for mobility. Other women continued to labor in the fields in a story of continuities rather than changes. Meanwhile, white men continued to beat, whip, and rape black women.

After emancipation, like their enslaved mothers and grandmothers before them, freed black women still found themselves having to perform a "double day" of paid labor followed by domestic chores. But continued racial oppression fostered a sense of racial solidarity among all African American women and men. The prospect of freedom encouraged black women collectively to organize to educate their families, foster literacy, and establish their own churches. Women had resisted their oppression, and those who survived the conflict looked to the future with hope and optimism.

Notes

1. Quoted in William Dusinberre, *Strategies for Survival: Recollections of Bondage in Antebellum Virginia* (Charlottesville and London: University of Virginia Press, 2009), 108–9.

2. Tena White and Eliza Hasty in the WPA narratives online: *South Carolina Narratives, Vol. 14, Part 4*, 198 and 256. Bessie Lawson in the WPA narratives online: *Arkansas Narratives, Vol. 2, Part 4*, 244–5.

3. Annie L. Burton, *Memories of Childhood's Slavery Days* (Boston: Ross Brown Publishing Company, 1909), 36. *Documenting the American South*, The University of North Carolina at Chapel Hill Library, http://docsouth.unc.edu/fpn/burton/menu.html.

4. Ellen Campbell in the WPA narratives online: *Georgia Narratives, Vol. 14, Part 4*, 225.

~

Epilogue

The Emancipation Proclamation of 1863, followed by the ending of the Civil War and the subsequent Thirteenth Amendment that abolished slavery within the United States, were momentous steps toward freedom. But in many respects the lives of black women changed little, despite their freedom. Released from the yoke of bondage, most freedwomen began to labor under a system of work known as sharecropping. Lacking in cash to purchase or rent farmland, sharecroppers paid their landlords with a share of the crops they grew. Although economically disadvantageous, sharecropping offered unique opportunities for African American women who sought economic independence while raising their families. Most freedwomen did not want to work as domestic servants in the homes of white women, but the low earnings of black men left many no other choice. Racism, poverty, and discrimination still loomed large in black women's lives, despite the legal, economic, and social changes that freedom had brought.

At the end of the war, four million emancipated slaves were in need of assistance. Rumors circulated that the government would provide each head of household, namely men, with "40 acres and a mule" to help freed families become self-sufficient, independent farmers. But these were rumors, and in the end freedpeople received little practical help from the government. The one exception was the Freedmen's Bureau, established in March 1865 to assist freedpeople with the transition from bondage to freedom. It negotiated labor contracts for freedpeople, established schools, assisted former slaves in search of family members from whom they had been separated, and provided medical help. However, the organization's role remained limited, largely due to lack of funding and white Southern opposition. White Southerners despised the bureau, regarding it as a symbol of Confederate defeat. With its focus on helping male heads of households, moreover, the bureau was of limited value to formerly enslaved women seeking to gain equality before the law, or to improve their economic input. During the Civil War, Union army officials had mistakenly assumed black women's total economic dependence on their husbands, an expectation that continued into the years following the war. In truth, black women, like many poor, white farm women, were obliged to supplement meager household incomes by working as sharecroppers or domestic servants. Freedwomen's lives continued to be characterized by racial oppression and gender discrimination. Freedom was undoubtedly a disappointment for freed women following the initial euphoria of emancipation.

Bondage was over, but blacks were still unable to participate fully in civic life. The Fourteenth and Fifteenth amendments to the Constitution promised African Americans equality under the law, granting them citizenship and giving African American men voting rights. However, the glory and joy of liberty ended rather abruptly for African Americans. State governments imposed discriminatory "Black Codes," limiting black rights to assemble, carry weapons, or own land, that rendered legal freedom rather meaningless. Moreover, emancipation did not equate with economic change. Despite a few brief wartime experiments giving confiscated Confederate lands to former slaves to farm, after the war, the federal government returned most of the land to the former owners.

Freedom did not bring about practical changes to the work lives of formerly enslaved women, and old patterns prevailed. Freedwomen continued to labor in fields belonging to whites, or serve as domestic servants in white women's homes just as they had done during slavery. Even the term *hiring out* survived into Reconstruction: Anne L. Burton and her sister, Caroline, were both "hired out" to white women to look after young children. While some freedwomen worked in white women's homes, others—mainly adult women with their own families—refused such offers of domestic work because it reminded them of slavery. Instead, they labored as sharecroppers, even though it plunged many African American families into debt. Sharecropping families normally worked for between one-third and one-quarter of the value of their crop, even with the Freedmen's Bureau assistance in negotiating their contracts. Short of cash, the sharecroppers often fell into the crop-lien system in which they put their small portion of the crop up as collateral for credit to buy tools, seed, food, and clothing for the year. The storeowners charged high interest rates for credit purchases and frequently cheated the black sharecroppers when they weighed their cotton crop as payment of the debt. To compound these problems, cotton prices fell in the late nineteenth century, and a combination of agricultural diseases and poor weather led to meager harvests. Thus, profits, if there were any, went to the white landowners, often their former masters, who rented their fields and cabins to African American families at a high price and overcharged them for supplies at the local stores.

But sharecropping cannot be measured in purely financial terms because the system had many benefits for African American women. Freedom from white supervision and the punishments, sexual or otherwise, they endured in the houses and fields of white masters and mistresses was crucial. Freedwomen also appreciated the sharecropping system because of its impact on their social and family lives. Sharecropping brought women control over their work schedules and pride in self-sufficiency. It allowed women to spend time with their husbands and children. Spouses previously forced by owners to live apart for most of the week because they belonged to different owners particularly relished the liberty to live and work together as a family. Husbands and wives had time to chat with each other, eat their meals with each other when they so desired, sleep together, and make love when they wanted. Moreover, in terms of social status, sharecropping was better than wage labor in the eyes of African Americans because it was relatively independent work. Adeline Grey proudly remembered her mother sharecropping, plowing every day "same as a man, for us chillun."[1] Laura Shelton's family sharecropped after the war, but when her father died they could not maintain their family's independence, and Shelton's mother had to return to domestic work, washing and ironing for white families.

Racial and gender discrimination remained a daily presence in black women's lives. Black women continued to live in fear of physical or sexual violence at the hands of white and black men. However, freedom offered African American women the opportunity to reconstruct their lives the way they wanted. While some rushed to legalize their marriages under U.S. law, Freedmen's Bureau records suggest that other women were anxious to leave behind the conflict and abuse of their marriages. In South Carolina, two women complained to bureau officials about their abusive husbands. Clarinda's husband beat her and was unfaithful. Laney's husband tried to justify his brutal attack on his wife by complaining about her lack of domesticity. He whipped Laney for "her laziness & being indifferent to his comfort or welfare, and not working, washing or mending his clothes, and for roaming about the country instead of being at home."[2] Former slaves Rose Williams and Lucy Skipwith linked emancipation to individual liberty and chose to leave their husbands.

Sometimes husbands abandoned their wives, who had a hard time supporting themselves or their children without financial assistance from their men. They turned to the Freedmen's Bureau to seek help from husbands who were unwilling—rather than unable—to provide for them. Sometimes these freedwomen asked the bureau to get the men to sign agreements to support them. At other times they requested that the bureau forcibly return absent husbands. Occasionally, women requested that they be granted property or land where their errant husbands now lived. Racial discrimination and unproductive sharecropping meant the men did not have much money. But freedwomen recognized the inherent contradiction and unfairness of a system in which they had to perform paid labor *and* shoulder family domestic responsibilities. Men needed to pull their weight as well.

Unmarried women faced additional hardships. The Freedmen's Bureau's reluctance to help single African American women made their lives even more difficult. Bureau officials worried that recognizing black female independence by giving single women aid might encourage more women to remain unmarried, which they worried could lead to sexual promiscuity among freedpeople. They preferred to distribute aid to male heads of households. But many formerly enslaved women were single because of forced separations, or because their husbands had died as a result of sickness or war. Thus, like many disabled, elderly, and orphaned freedpeople, these African American women who found themselves without kin networks were especially vulnerable to poverty and destitution because they were unable to turn to the bureau for support.

Negotiating work and marriage consumed much of freedwomen's time. But their legacy of hard work and courage during adversity also led formerly enslaved women to seek self-improvement and a better life for their children after the Civil War. Legal freedom created an opportunity for women to acquire social status and prestige among their peers, and these new identities challenged white notions of racial inferiority. Primarily, women's efforts revolved around the creation of independent African American churches and the establishment of schools to educate their children. Formerly enslaved in North Carolina, Harriet Jacobs and her daughter settled in Savannah, Georgia, after the war in order to set up a school to assist freedpeople. Likewise, Susie King Taylor, a former slave who lived as a contraband on the Union-occupied Georgia Sea Islands, later returned to her home city of Savannah to set up an educational academy in her house. Susie taught basic literacy to both children and adults. Formerly enslaved women found these examples to be positive role models. A few illiterate freedwomen were inspired to become assistants to black female teachers, and some were eventually able to enter the profession themselves.

During slavery it was unusual for enslaved women to read and write, although some had achieved a basic level of literacy despite legal prohibitions against the education of slaves. This denial of basic education made the thirst for knowledge following emancipation all the more urgent. Freedmen and women quenched this thirst by establishing independent schools, fund-raising for them, and studying by candlelight at home, even after an arduous day's labor. Women networked and organized to help themselves and their communities. Like African American churches, schools formed the backbone of freedpeople's independence, and women fought hard for the creation and preservation of these institutions in the face of ever growing white hostility and racism. White pressure on the federal government resulted in the defunding of the Freedmen's Bureau by 1872. Thereafter, the political compromise of 1877 effectively ended what white Southerners termed "the Northern occupation" of the South, meaning that African Americans would have to rely primarily on themselves to better their lives. Freedwomen played important roles in these self-help efforts.

Throughout slavery, the Civil War era, and subsequent freedom, there existed certain continuities in the lives of black women. Strong and resilient, they worked a "double day"—performing paid labor before tending to home and family. Slaveholders never reconciled whether their enslaved women were primarily laborers or reproducers, so they exploited them as both. Likewise, freedwomen themselves grappled with their identity as they moved from bondage to freedom. African American women continued to perform multiple roles as both workers and homemakers. But their efforts to protect themselves and the interests of their immediate families provided enduring strategies to cope with the challenges in the United States that remain to this day.

Notes

1. Adeline Grey quoted in Marli F. Weiner, *Mistresses and Slaves: Plantation Women in South Carolina 1830–1880* (Urbana and Chicago: University of Illinois Press, 1998), 207.

2. See Leslie Schwalm, *A Hard Fight for We: Women's Transition from Slavery to Freedom in South Carolina* (Urbana and Chicago: University of Illinois Press, 1997), 234, 260–6, for these and other examples of domestic violence inflicted by slave men upon enslaved women.

~

Documents

African Weddings

Olaudah Equiano's 1789 autobiography provides a unique glimpse of women's everyday life in precolonial West Africa. Here he describes a typical marriage ceremony, the importance of exchanging gifts upon entering wedlock, and the festivities that followed wedding ceremonies. His testimony illustrates similarities between African marriages and those of women enslaved in America.

Their mode of marriage is thus: —both parties are usually betrothed when young by their parents, (though I have known the males to betroth themselves). On this occasion a feast is prepared, and the bride and bridegroom stand up in the midst of all their friends, who are assembled for the purpose while he declares that she is thenceforth to be looked upon as his wife, and that no other person is to pay any address to her. This is also immediately proclaimed in the vicinity, on which the bride retires from the assembly. Sometime after, she is brought home to her husband, and then another feast is made, to which the relations of both parties are invited: her parents then deliver her to the bridegroom, accompanied with a number of blessings, and at the same time they tie round her waist a cotton string the thickness of a goose-quill, which none but married women are permitted to wear: she is now considered completely his wife; and at this time the dowry is given to the new married pair, which generally consists of land, slaves, cattle, household goods, and implements of husbandry. These are offered by the friends of both parties; besides which the parents of the bridegroom present gifts to those of the bride, whose property she is looked upon before marriage, but after it she is esteemed the sole property of her husband. The ceremony now being ended, the festival begins, which is celebrated with bonfires, and loud acclamations of joy, accompanied with music and dancing.

—Olaudah Equiano, *The Interesting Narrative of the Life of Olaudah Equiano*, edited by Angelo Costanzo (Ontario: Broadview, 2004 [1789]), 47–48.

Mary Prince's Recollections of Caribbean Slavery

West Indian slave Mary Prince recalled the brutality of Caribbean slavery, where enslaved women suffered many cruel punishments at the hands of their masters, mistresses, and overseers. Women also endured hard physical labor while growing sugarcane and other types of produce on the Caribbean islands. Prince describes her ordeal while harvesting salt in the blistering heat of the Caribbean. Typically, Mary and the other slaves working on the islands slept together in long, dormitory-style buildings. In contrast, enslaved women in North America lived either with their families in their own cabins or their owners' "Big House."

The next morning my mistress set about instructing me in my tasks. She taught me to do all sorts of household work; to wash and bake, pick cotton and wool, and wash floors, and cook. And she taught me (how can I ever forget it!) more things than these; she caused me to know the exact difference between the smart of the rope, the cart-whip, and the cow-skin, when applied to my naked body by her own cruel hand. And there was scarcely any punishment more dreadful than the blows I received on my face and head from her hard heavy fist. She was a fearful woman, and a savage mistress to her slaves.

My new master [in Turks Island in the Caribbean] was one of the owners or holders of the salt ponds, and he received a certain sum for every slave what worked upon his premises, whether they were young or old. This sum allowed him out of the profits arising from the salt works. I was immediately sent to work in the salt water with the rest of the slaves. This work was perfectly new to me I was given a half barrel and a shovel, and had to stand up to my knees in the water, from four o'clock in the morning till nine, when we were given some Indian corn boiled in water, which we were obliged to swallow as fast as we could for fear the rain should come on and melt the salt. We were then called again to our tasks, and worked through the heat of the day; the sun flaming upon our heads like fire, and raising salt blisters in those parts which were not completely covered. Our feet and legs, from standing in the salt water for so many hours, soon became full of dreadful boils, which eat down in some cases to the very bone, afflicting the sufferers with great torment. We came home at twelve; ate our corn soup, called *blawly*, as fast as we could, and went back to our employment till dark at night. We then shoveled up the salt in large heaps, and went down to the sea, where we washed the pickle from our limbs, and cleaned the barrows and shovels from the salt. When we returned to the house, our master gave us each our allowance of raw Indian corn, which we pounded in a mortar and boiled in water for our suppers.

We slept in a long shed, divided into narrow slips, like the stall used for cattle. Boards fixed upon stakes, driven into the ground, without mat or covering, were our only beds. On Sundays, after we had washed the salt bags, and done other work required of us, we went into the bush and cut the long soft grass, of which we made trusses for our legs and feet to rest upon, for they were so full of salt boils that we could get no rest lying there on the bare boards. Though we worked from morning till night, there was no satisfying Mr. D—. I hoped, when I left Capt. I—, that I should have been better off, but I found it was but going from one butcher to another. There was this difference between them: my former master used to beat me while raging and foaming with passion; Mr. D— was usually quite calm. . . . Nothing could touch his hard heart—neither sighs, nor tears, nor prayers, nor streaming blood; he was deaf to our cries, and careless of our sufferings. Mr. D— has often stripped me naked, hung me up by the wrists, and beat me with the cow-skin, with his own hand, till my body was raw with gashes.

Mary Prince, *The History of Mary Prince, A West Indian Slave* (London: Penguin, 2004 [1831]), 19–20.

Virginia Laws from the 1660s

Colonial Virginia led the way in formulating and enacting laws defining the status of enslaved women. By decreeing that children follow the status of their mothers, Virginia paved the way for white men's sexual exploitation of enslaved women in order to provide them with valuable enslaved offspring. Virginia also forbade interracial sexual liaisons, outlawed enslaved baptism as a means of achieving freedom, and passed laws permitting the physical punishment of slaves. By subjecting freed black women to taxes from which white women were exempt, Virginia also led the way in formalizing laws that increasingly separated black people from whites.

Whereas some doubts have arisen whether children got by any Englishman upon a Negro woman should be slave or free, *be it therefore enacted and declared by this present Grand Assembly,* that all children born in this country shall be held bond or free only according to the condition of the mother; *And* that if any Christian shall commit fornication with a Negro man or woman, he or she so offending shall pay double the fines imposed by the former act. (December 1662).

Whereas some doubts have risen whether children that are slaves by birth, and by the charity and piety of their owners made partakers of the blessed sacrament of baptism, should by virtue of their baptism be made free, *it is enacted and declared by this Grand Assembly, and the authority thereof*, that the conferring of baptism does not alter the condition of the person as to his bondage or freedom; that diverse masters, freed from this doubt may more carefully endeavor the propagation of Christianity by permitting children, though slaves, or chose of greater growth if capable, to be admitted to that sacrament. (September 1667).

Whereas it has been questioned whether servants running away may be punished with corporal punishment by their master or magistrate, since the act already made gives the master satisfaction by prolonging their time by service, *it is declared and enacted by this Assembly* that moderate corporal punishment inflicted by master or magistrate upon a runaway servant shall not deprive the master of the satisfaction allowed by the law, the one being as necessary to reclaim them from persisting in that idle course as the other is just to repair the damages sustained by the master. (September 1668).

Whereas the only law in force for the punishment of refractory servants resisting their master, mistress, or overseer cannot be inflicted upon Negroes, nor the obstinacy of many of them be suppressed by other than violent means, *be it enacted and declared by this Grand Assembly* if any slave resists his master (or other by his master's order correcting him) and by the extremity of the correction should chance to die, that his death shall not be accounted a felony, but the master (or that other person appointed by the master to punish him) be acquitted from molestation, since it cannot be presumed that premeditated malice (which alone makes murder a felony) should induce any man to destroy his own estate. (October 1669).

—All cited in William Waller Hening, *Statutes at Large; Being a Collection of All the Laws of Virginia*, *Vol. 11* (Richmond, VA, 1809–23), 170, 260, 266, 270. Accessed at www.swarthmore.edu/SocSci/ bdorsey1/41docs/24-sla.html.

Whereas some doubts have arisen whether negro women set free were still to be accompted tithable according to a former act, *it is declared by this general assembly* that negro women, though permitted to enjoy their freedome yet ought not in all respects to be admitted to a full fruition of the exemptions and impunities of the English, and are still liable to payment of taxes.

—1668 Virginia Statute, quoted in Kathleen M. Brown, *Good Wives, Nasty Wenches, and Anxious Patriarchs: Gender, Race, and Power in Colonial Virginia* (Chapel Hill and London: University of North Carolina Press, 1996), 122.

Enslaved Weddings in Colonial Times

In 1731, John Brickell commented on an enslaved wedding, emphasizing that the exchanging of gifts remained an important symbol of wedlock.

Their [slaves] *Marriages* are generally performed amongst themselves, there being very little ceremony used upon that Head; for the Man makes the Woman a Present, such as a *Brass Ring*, or some other Toy, which if she accepts of becomes his Wife; but if ever they part from each other, which frequently happens, upon any little Disgust, she returns his Present: These kinds of Contracts no longer binding them, than the woman keeps the pledge give her.

—John Brickell, 1731. Quoted in Sylvia R. Frey and Betty Wood, *Come Shouting to Zion: African American Protestantism in the American South and British Caribbean to 1830* (Chapel Hill and London: University of North Carolina Press, 1998), 50.

Colonial Enslaved Women Who Ran Away

White people increasingly made it difficult for enslaved people to flee from their owners; nonetheless, black women escaped slavery. They sometimes escaped with their families, and more rarely (as the runaway advertisement from the South Carolina Gazette *illustrates) in large groups, especially during the colonial era, when escape proved easier for slaves than in subsequent years.*

Runaway . . . on the 11th of July last a negro Fellow named Mingo, about 40 years old, and his wife Quane, a sensible wench about 20, with her child a Boy about 3 years old, all this Country born: Also Cudjoe a sensible Coro-mantee Negro Fellow about 45 years old, stutters, and his wife Dinah an Ebo wench that speaks very good English, with her two children a Boy about 8 years old, and a Girl of about 18 months.

—Runaway slave advertisement in the *South Carolina Gazette*, September 1747. Quoted in Jennifer L. Morgan, *Laboring Women: Reproduction and Gender in New World Slavery* (Philadelphia: University of Pennsylvania Press, 2004), 190.

The Sale and Separation of Enslaved Women

The enforced separation of enslaved women from their loved ones constituted one of the cruelest blows of American slavery. Here, female WPA respondents remember the heartbreak of sales. Following the death of her mistress's father-in-law, Mintie Maria Miller was sold on an open market where she felt degraded, like an animal. When Maria lashed out at a potential purchaser, the man refused to buy her. Eventually, Maria was sold twice on the same day. Fannie Moore, like many WPA respondents, spoke to her interviewer about sales only in general terms, but she similarly commented on the objectification of enslaved women. Emma L. Howard sang a song to her interviewer that expressed enslaved women's fear of being sold "down south," while Maria Hervey described how slaveholders separated her husband from his mother when he was a small child. She also explained how overseers beat slaves who failed to sell on the auction block. Sarah Gudger remembered enslaved people being sold to speculators while their mothers and wives remained, crying. In her autobiography, Harriet Jacobs wondered why enslaved women ever allowed themselves to fall in love when spouses might be wrenched away at any moment by masters representing "the hand of violence."

I was born in Alabama in 1852 in Tuscaloosa and my mammy's name was Hannah, but I don't know my pappy's name. When I was still pretty little my brother and uncle and aunt and mother was sold and me with 'em. Dr. Massie brung us to Texas in an oxcart but my sister has to stay with the old mistress and that the last I ever seen my sister. She was four year old then. . . . Then they says they gwine sell me, 'cause Miss. Nancy's father-in-law dies and they got rid of some of us. She [Miss. Nancy] didn't want to sell me so she tell me to be sassy and no one would buy me. They takes me to Houston and to the market and a man call George Fraser sells de slaves. The market was a open house, more like a shed. We all stands to one side till our turn comes. They wasn't nothin' else you could do. They stands me up on a block of wood and a man bid me in. I felt mad. You see I was young then, too young to know better. I don't know what they sold me for, but the man what bought me made me open my mouth while he looks at my teeth. They all done us that-a-way. Sells us like you sell a hoss. Then my old master bids me goodbye and tried to give me a dog, but I 'members what Miss. Nancy done say and I sassed him and slapped the dog out of his hand. So the man what bought me say, "When one o-clock come you got to sell her 'gain, she's sassy. If she done me that way I'd kill her." So they sells me twice the same day. They was two sellin's that day.

—Mintie Maria Miller in the WPA narratives online: *Texas Narratives, Vol. 16, Part 3,* 85–86. Library of Congress, http://memory.loc.gov/ammem/snhtml/snhome.html.

It was a trubble sight to see de speculators come to de plantation. Dey would go through de fields and buy de slaves dey wanted. Marse Jim nebber sell pappy or mammy or any ob dey chillun. He allus like pappy. When de speculator come all de slaves start a shakin'. No one know who is goin'. Den sometime dey take 'em an' sell 'em on de block. De "breed woman" always bring mo' money den de res', ebben de men. When dey put her on de block dey put all her chillun around her to show folks how fas she can hab chillun.

—Fannie Moore, age eighty-eight, *Born in Slavery: Slave Narratives from the Federal Writers' Project, 1936–1938*, Library of Congress.

When she sold her family nebber see her agin. She nebber know how many chillun she hab. Some time she hab colored children an' sometime white. Tain't no use to say anything case effen she do she jes git whipped.

—Fannie Moore in the WPA narratives online: *North Carolina Narratives*, Vol. 11, Part 2, 131. Library of Congress.

Mammy, is Ole' Massa gwin'er sell us tomorrow? Yes, my chile.
Whar he gwin'er sell us?
Way down South in Georgia.

Dat was one of de saddest songs we sung en durin' slavery days . . . it always
did make me cry.

—Emma L. Howard in the WPA narratives online: *Alabama Narratives*, Vol. 1, 211. Library of Congress.

My father's white people were named Taylor'—old Job Taylor's folks. They
lived in Tennessee. . . . My mother said they had a block to put the colored
people and their children on and they would tell them to tell people what
they could do when the people asked them. It would just be a lot of lies. And
some of them wouldn't do it. One or two of the colored folks they would sell
and they would carry the others back. When they got them back they would
lock them up and they would have the overseers beat them, and bruise them,
and knock them 'round and say "Yes, you can't talk, huh? You can't tell
people what you can do?" But they got a beating for lying, and they would uh
got one if they hadn't lied, most likely. They used to take pregnant women
and dig a hole in the ground and put their stomachs in it and whip them. . . .
They sold his [Marie's husband's] mother and two children and kept him. He
went into the house crying and old mis' gave him some biscuits and butter.
You see, they didn't give them biscuits then. That was the same as giving him
candy. She said "Old mis' goin' to give you some good biscuits and some butter." He never did hear from his mother until after freedom. Some thought
about him and wrote him a letter for her. There was a man here who was
from North Carolina and my husband got to talking with him and he was
going back and he knew my husband's mother and his brother and he said he
would write to my husband if my husband would write him a letter and give
it to him to give to his mother. He did it and his mother sent him an answer.
He would have gone to see her but he didn't have money enough then. The
bank broke and he lost what little he had saved. He corresponded with her
till he died. But he never did get to see her any more.

—Marie E. Hervey in the WPA narratives online: *Arkansas Narratives*, Vol. 2, Part 3, 231–2. Library
of Congress.

Wahn't none o' de slaves offen ouh plantation ebbah sold, but de ones on de
othah plantation ob Marse William wah. Oh, dat wah a terrible time! All de
slaves be in de field, plowin', hoein', singin' in de boilin' sun. ole Marse he
cum t'ru de field wif a man call de specalater. Dey walk round jes' lookin',
jes' lookin'. All de da'kies know whus dis mean. Dey didn' dare look up, jes'
wok right on. Den de specalater he see who de want. He talk to Ole Marse,
den dey slaps de han'cuffs on him an tak him away to de cotton country.

Oh, dem wah awful times! When de specalater wah ready to go wif de slaves, effen dey wha enny whu didn' wanta go, he thrash em, den he tie em 'hind waggin an' mek em run till dey fall on de groun', den he trash em till dey say dey go 'thout no trubble. Sometime some of dem run 'way an cum back t'de plantation, den it wah harder on dem den befoah. When de da'kies wen'

—Sarah Gudger, Age 121, *Born in Slavery: Slave Narratives from the Federal Writers' Project, 1936–1938*, Library of Congress.

t'dinnah de ole niggah mammy she say whar am sich an' sich. None ob de othahs wannah tell huh. But when she sees dem look down to de groun' she jes' say: "De specalater, de specalater." Den de teahs roll down huh cheeks, cause mebbe it huh son o' husban' an she know she nebbeh see 'em agin. Mebbe dey leaves babies t'home, mebbe jes' pappy an' mammy. Oh, mah Lawdy, Mah old Boss wah mean, but he nebbah sen' us to de cotton country.

—Sarah Gudger in the WPA narratives online: *North Carolina Narratives, Vol. 11, Part 1*, 354–5. Library of Congress.

Why does the slave ever love? Why allow the tendrils of the heart to twine around objects which may at any moment by wrenched away by the hand of violence? When separations come by the hand of death the pious soul can bow in resignation, and say, "Not my will, but thine be done, O' Lord!" But when the ruthless hand of man strikes the blow, regardless of the misery he causes, it is hard to be submissive. I did not reason thus when I was a young girl. Youth will be youth I loved, and I indulged the hope that the dark clouds around me would turn out a bright lining. I forgot that in the land of my birth the shadows are too dense for light to penetrate. A land

> Where laughter and not mirth; nor thought the mind;
> Nor words a language; nor e'en men mankind.
> Where cried reply to curses, shrieks to blows,
> And each is tortured in his separate hell.

—Harriet Jacobs, *Incidents in the Life of a Slave Girl* (New York: Dover, 2001 [1861]), 33–34.

Memories of Enslaved Culture and Religion

Formerly enslaved women interviewed by the WPA had strong memories of their social lives as slaves during antebellum times. Frequently, they recalled parties where young slave women could dress up, meet young men, and partake in courtship rituals, including singing and dancing, as Anna Wright and Fannie Berry remembered. These social events often had an important religious component, and courtships, not surprisingly, led to weddings. Enslaved wedding ceremonies constituted important community celebrations that often had a religious component. Religion itself was an important part of enslaved women's lives, although Alice Sewell and Lucretia Alexander both rather resented their white preachers' views. Instead, they recalled in a favorable light the secret meetings slaves held in isolation, away from the prying eyes of whites.

Dere must of been 'bout two hundret slaves, 'cordin' ter de number of cabins. De slaves worked hard in de fiel's but unless de work wus pushin' dey had sadday evenin' off ter go a-fishin an do anything de wanted ter do. Two or three times a year Marse James let dem have a dance an' invite all in de neighbourhood slaves. Dey had corn shuckin's ever' fall an' de other slaves cud come ter dem. De candy pullin's wus a big affair wid de niggers. Dey's come from all over de neighbourhood ter cook de lasses [molasses] an' pull de candy. While de candy cooled dey'd play drappin' de handkerchief an' a heap of other games. De courtin' couples liked dese games 'case dey could set out or plan an' court all dey pleased. Dey often make up dere min's ter ax de marster iffen dey could marry, too, at dese parties.

De weddin's wus somethin' fine, believe me. De niggers dressed lak a white folks weddin' an' de circuit parson married dem in de big house parlour. De marster an' de missus wus dere, an' dey always gived presents ter de bride too. Atter de ceremony wus over dar'd be a feas' an' a dance. Most likely dar'd be a heap of noise. I've heard mammy tell of seberal big weddin's. Mammy tol' me date Marse James wus a very religious man, an' dat wus why de preacher married de slaves, an' why he made all of de slaves go ter church on Sunday an' say de blessin' at meal times.

My pappy wus named Tom, an' he worked in de fiel's fer Marse James. Hit wus pappy dat haul up de watermelons in de wagin. . . . Marse James raise a plenty melons fer all of de slaves an' he raise plenty of hogs ter eat de rines. De slaves uster have a watermelon slicin' 'bout once a week an' sometimes dey'd invite de neighbors in.

—Anna Wright in the WPA narratives online: *North Carolina Narratives, Vol. 11, Part 2*, 421–3. Library of Congress.

I wuz one slave dat de poor white man had his match. . . . One tried to throw me but he couldn't. We tusseled an' knocked over chairs an' when I got a grin I stratched his face all to pieces; an dar wuz no more bothering Fannie from him; but oh, honey, some slaves would be beat up so, when they resisted. . . . Us colored women had to go through a plenty, I tell you. . . . Now Miss Sue, take up. I jes' like to tell you, honey, 'bout dem days ob slavery; 'cause you look like you wan'ta hear all 'bout 'em. . . . Used to go over to de Saunders place fo' dancin'. Musta been hundred slaves over that, an' they always had de bes' dances. Mos' times fo' de dance dey had Dennis to play de banjer. Dennis had a twisted arm, an' he couldn't do much work, but he sho' could pick dat banjer. Gals would put on dey spare dress ef day had one, an' men would put a clean shirt on. Gals always tried to fix up fo' partyin' even ef dey ain't got nothin' but a piece of ribbon to tie in dey hair. Mos' times wear yo' shoes to de dance an' den take 'em off. Dem ole hard shoes make too much noise, an' hurt yo' feet. Couldn't do no steppin' in dem field shoes.

—Fannie Berry in the WPA narratives online: *Virginia Narratives, Vol. 17*, 1–6. Library of Congress.

I ain't never been in a school house in my life and I never did learn how to read or write. . . . Dey didn't 'low us to sing on our plantation 'cause if we did we just sing ourselves happy and git to shouting and dat would settle de work, yes mam. . . . Dey did 'low us to go to church on Sunday about two miles down de public road, and dey hired a white preacher to preach to us. He never did tell us nothing about be good servants, pick up old masse and old misses' things about de place, and don't steal no chickens or pigs and don't lie 'bout nothing. Den dey baptize you and call dat, you got religion. Never did say nothing 'bout a slave dying and going to heaven. When we die, dey bury us next day and you is just like any of de other cattle dying on de place. Dat's all 'tis to it and all 'tis of you. You is jest dead dat's all. De old lady dat raised my mother, she was a black mammy. She dine all de burying of de niggers, said de funeral sayings by herself. She knew it by heart. Dey swapped my grandmother away cause she didn't bear children like dey wanted her to. . . . We used to slip off in de woods in de old slave days on Sunday evening way down in de swamps to sing and pray to our own liking. We prayed for dis day of freedom. We come from four and five miles away to pray together to God dat if we don't live to see it, do please let our chillun live to see a better day and be free, so dat dey can give honest and fair service to de Lord and all mankind everywhere. And we'd sing "Our little meetin's 'bout to break, chillun must part. We got to part in body, but hope not in mind. Our little meetin's 'bout to break." Den we used to sing "We walk about and shake hands, fare you well my sisters I am going home."

—Alice Sewell in the WPA narratives online: *Missouri Narratives, Vol. 10*, 301–6. Library of Congress.

They would make the slaves work till twelve o'clock on Sunday, and then they would let them go to church. The first time I was sprinkled, a white preacher did it; I think his name was William. The preacher would preach to the white folks in the forenoon and to the colored folks in the evening. The white folks had them hired. One of them preachers was named Hackett; another, Williams; and another, Gowan. There was five of them but I just remember them three. One man used to hold the slaves so late that they had to go to the church dirty from their work. They would be sweaty and smelly. So the preacher 'buked him 'bout it. That was old man Bill Rose.

The niggers didn't go to the church building; the preacher came and preached to them in their quarters. He's just say, "Serve your masters. Don't steal your master's turkey. Don't steal your master's chickens. Don't steal your master's hawgs. Don't steal your master's meat. Do whatsomever your master tells you to do." Same old thing all the time. My father would have church in dwelling houses and they had to whisper. My mother was dead and I would go with him. Sometimes they would have church at his house. That would be when they would want a real meetin' with some real preachin'. It would have to be durin' the week nights. You couldn't tell the difference between Baptists and Methodists then. They was all Christians. I never saw them turn nobody down at the communion, but I have heard of it. I never saw them turn no pots down neither; but I have heard of that. They used to sing their songs in a whisper and pray in a whisper. That was a prayer-meeting from house to house once or twice – once or twice a week.

—Lucretia Alexander in the WPA narratives online: *Arkansas Narratives, Vol. 2, Part 1*, 35. Library of Congress.

Enslaved Weddings in Antebellum Times

By antebellum times, "abroad" marriages—those in which enslaved spouses belonged to different owners—had become more common. Louisa Davis, a former slave in South Carolina, recalled her joy at her husband's visits when his owner granted him a pass.

Just who I b'long to when a baby? I'll leave dat for de white folks to tell, but old Marster Jim Lemon buy us all; pappy, mammy, and thee chillun: Jake, So-phie and me. De white folks I furst b'long to refuse to sell 'less Marse Jim buy de whole family. . . . My pappy rise to be foreman on de place and was much trusted, but he plowed and plowed. Just de same, mammy say maybe harder.

Den one springtime de flowers git be blooming, de hens to cackling, and de guineas to patarocking. Sam come along when I was out in de yard wid de baby. He fust talk to de baby, and I asked him if de baby wasn't pretty. He say, "Yes, but not as pretty as you is, Louisa." I looks at Sam, and dat kind of foolishness wind up in a weddin'. De white folks allowed us to be married on de back piazza, and Reverend Boggs performed de ceremony.

My husband was a slave of de Sloans and didn't get to see me as often as he wanted to; and of course, as de housemaid then. Dere was times I couldn't meet him, clandestine like he want me. Us dat some grief over dat, but he got a pass twice a week from his master, Marse Tommie Sloan, to come to see me. . . . Dat nigger was timid as a rabbit wid me when us furst git married. Shucks, let's talk 'bout something else. . . . Sam was a field hand and drive de wagon way to Charleston once a year wid cotton, and always bring back something pretty for me.

—Louisa Davis in the WPA narratives online: *South Carolina Narratives, Vol. 14, Part 1*, 299–300. Library of Congress.

Recollections of Pregnancy, Work, and Health Care

Some female WPA respondents remembered their masters forcing them to work until the time they gave birth, although others, like Adeline Jackson's master, gave pregnant women lighter duties to perform. Ryer Emmanuel's master gave his female slaves a month off after giving birth. Thereafter, an elderly female slave looked after enslaved women's babies and children. Similarly, Fannie Moore remembered the traditional health care of senior enslaved women on her North Carolina plantation.

Doctor Henry Gibson was our doctor. . . . Yes sir, at certain times we worked long and hard, and you had to be 'ticular. De only whipping I got was for chopping down a good corn stalk near a stumpy in a new ground. Marster never sold a slave, but swaps were made wid kin people to advantage, slaves' wives and husbands sometimes. I never learned to read or write. I went to White poplar Springs Church, de Baptist church my mistress 'tended. Yes, Women in de family way worked up to near de time, but guess Dr. Gibson knowed his business. Just befo' de time, they was took out and put in de cardin' and spinnin' rooms.

—Adeline Jackson in the WPA narratives online: *South Carolina Narratives, Vol. 14, Part 3*, 2–3. Library of Congress.

Oh my Lord, child, I ain't know nothing bout slavery time no more then we was just little kids livin dere on de white people plantation. I was just a little yearlin' child den, I say. Been bout six years old in slavery time. . . . I was a big little girl stayin' in old Massa yard in dem days, but I wasn' big enough to do nothing in de house no time. . . . Wouldn' make dem do no heavy work right to start wid. But dem what was older, dey had to work in de field. I reckon dey would be workin; just about like dey is now from sunrise in de morning till sunset in de evenin'.

Always when a woman would get in de house [to have a baby], old Massa would let her leave off work then stay dere to de house a month till she get mended in de body way. Den she would have to carry de child to de big house en get back in de field to work. Oh, dey had a old woman in de yard to de house to stay dere en mind all de plantation chillun till night come, while dey parents was workin'. Dey would let de chillun go home wid dey mammy to spend de night en den she would have to march dem right back to de yard de next morning. We didn' do nothin', but play 'bout de yard dere en eat what de woman feed us. Yes'um, dey would carry us dere when de women would be gwine to work. Be dere fore sunrise. Would give us three meals a day cause de old women always give us supper fore us mammy come out de fields dat evenin'. Dem bigger ones, dey would give dem claber en boil peas en collards sometimes. Would give de little babies boil pea soup en gruel en suck bottle. Yes, mam, de old woman had to mind all de yearlin' chillun en de babies too. Dat all her business was. I recollects her name, it been Lettie. Would string us little wooden bowls on de floor in a long row en us would get down dere and drink just like was pigs. Oh, she would give us a iron spoon to taste wid, but us wouldn' never want it.

—Ryer Emmanuel in the WPA narratives online: *South Carolina Narratives, Vol. 14, Part 2*, 11–13. Library of Congress.

Nowadays, when I heah folks a' growlin an' a grumblin bout not habbin this an' that I jes think what would they have done effen they be brought up on de Moore plantation. De Moore plantation b'long to Marse Jim Moore, in Moore, South Carolina. De Moores had own de same plantation and de same niggers and dey children for yeahs back. When Marse Jim's pappy die he leave de whole thing to Marse Jim, effen he take care of his mammy. She shore was a rip-jack. She say niggers didn't need nothin' to eat. Dey jes like animals, not like other folks. She whip me, many time, wif a cowhide, till I was black and blue.

My granny she cook for us chillens while our mammy away in de fiel. Dey wasn't much cookin' to do. Jes make co'n pone and bring in de milk. She hab wig wooden bowl wif enough wooden spoons to go roun'. She put de milk in de bowl and break it up. Den she put de bowl in de middle of de flo' and all de chillun grab a spoon.

My mammy she work in de fiel' all day and piece and quilt all night. Den she hab to spin enough thread to make four cuts for de white fo'ks ebber night. Why sometime I nebber go to bed. Hab to hold de light for her to see by. She hab to piece quilts for de white folks too. . . . I never see how may mammy stan' sech ha'd work. She stan' up fo' her chillun tho'. De ol' overseeah he hate my mammy, case she fight him for beati' her chillun. Why she git more whuppins for dat than enathin' else. She hab twelve chillun. I member I see de three oldes' stan' in de snow up to dey knees to split rails, while de overseeah stan off an' grin.

My mammy grieve lots over brothah George, who die wif de fever. Granny she doctah him as bes' she could, evah time she git way from white folks kitchen. My mammy nevah git chance to see him, 'cept when she git home in de evenin' George he jes lie. One day I look at him an' he had sech a peaceful look on his face, I think he sleep and jes let him lone. Long in de evening I think I try to wake him. I touch him one de face but he was dead. Mammy nebber know till she come at night. Pore mammy she kneel by de bed an' cry her heart out.

Folks back den never heah tell of all de ailments de folks hab now. Dey war no doctahs. Jes use roots and bark for teas of all kinds. My ole granny uster make tea out o' dogwood bark an' give it to us chillun when we have a cold, else she make a tea outen wild cherry bark, pennyroil, or hoarhound. My goodness but dey was bitter. We do mos' anythin' to git out a takin' de tea, but twarnt no use granny jes git you by de collar hol' you nose and you jes swallow it or get strangled. When de baby hab de colic she gits rats vein and make a syrup an' out a little sugar in it an' boil it. Den soon as it cold she give it to de baby. For stomach ache she give us snake root. Sometime she make tea, other time she jes cut it up in little pieces and make you eat one or two ob den. When you hab fever she wrap you up in cabbage leaves or ginsang leaves, dis made de fever do. When de fever got too bad she take de hoofs offen de hog dat had been killed and parch em' in de ashes and den she beat em' up and make a tea. Dis was de most tubble of all.

—Fannie Moore in the WPA narratives online: *North Carolina Narratives*, *Vol. 11*, *Part 2*, 128–31, 134–5. Library of Congress.

Sexual Assaults on Enslaved Women

Some female slaves endured horrific sexual assaults at the hands of white men. Sometimes the women's owners were the aggressors; sometimes they were other members of slaveholding families. Women such as Harriet Jacobs sometimes faced years of abuse at the hands of their masters while their mistresses responded with jealousy or rage. Former slaves felt understandably uncomfortable about conveying such private matters to white WPA interviewers and tended to describe the interracial relationships of other enslaved women and their masters, as Mary Reynolds explained. Other respondents, including Minnie Fulkes, remembered assaults at the hands of white overseers. WPA interviewee Rose Williams described how her master forced her to partake in an intimate relationship with a male slave against her will, but this kind of testimony is very rare.

But I now entered my fifteenth year—a sad epoch in the life of a slave girl. My master began to whisper foul words in my ear. Young as I was, I could not remain ignorant of their import. I tried to tear them with indifference or contempt. The master's age, my extreme youth, and the fear that his conduct would be reported to my grandmother, made him bear this treatment for many months. He was a crafty man, and resorted to many ways to accomplish his purposes. Sometimes he had stormy, terrific ways that made his victims tremble; sometimes he assumed a gentleness that he thought must surely subdue. Of the two, I preferred his stormy moods, although they left me trembling. He tried his utmost to corrupt the pure principles my grandmother had instilled. He peopled my young mind with unclean images, such as only a vile monster could think of. I turned from him with disgust and hatred. But he was my master. I was compelled to live under the same roof with him—where I saw a man forty years my senior daily violating the most sacred commandments of nature. He told me I was his property; that I must be subject to his will in all things. My soul revolted against the mean tyranny. But where could I turn for protection? No matter whether the slave girl be as black as ebony or as fair as her mistress. In either case, there is no shadow of law to protect her from insult, from violence, or even from death; all these are inflicted by fiends who bear the shape of men. The mistress, who ought to protect the helpless victim, has no other feelings towards her but those of jealousy and rage.

Mrs. Flint possessed the key to her husband's character before I was born. She might have used this knowledge to counsel and to screen the young and the innocent among her slaves; but for them she had no sympathy. They were the objects of her constant suspicion and malevolence. She watched her husband with unceasing vigilance; but he was well practiced in means to evade it. . . . I had entered my sixteenth year, and every day it became more and more apparent that my presence was intolerable to Mrs. Flint. Angry words frequently passed between her and her husband. He had never punished me himself, and he would not allow anybody else to punish me. In that respect, she was never satisfied; not in her angry moods, no terms were too vile for her to bestow on me. Yet I, whom she detested so bitterly, had far more pity for her than he had, whose duty it was to make her life happy. I never wronged her, or wished to wrong her; and one word of kindness from her would have brought me to her feet.

—Southern women often marry a man knowing he is the father of many little slaves. They do not trouble themselves about it. They regard such children as property, as marketable as the pigs on the plantation; and it is seldom that they do not make them aware of this by passing them into the slave trader's hands as soon as possible, and thus getting them out of their sight. I am glad to say there are some honorable exceptions. —Harriet Jacobs, *Incidents in the Life of a Slave Girl* (New York: Dover, 2001 [1861]), 26, 29, 33.

Once massa goes to Baton Rouge and brung back a yaller girl dressed in fine style. She was a seamster nigger. He builds her a house 'way from the quarters an she done fine sewin' for the whites. Us niggers knowed the doctor [their master] took a black woman quick as he did a white and took any on his place he wanted, and he took them often, But mostly the chillun born on the place looked like niggers. Aunt Cheyney allus say four of hers was masses, but he didn't give them no mind. But this yaller gal breeds so fast and gits a mess of white young 'uns. . . . Once two of them goes down the hill to the doll house where the Kilpatrick children [master's children] am playin'. They wants to go in the dollhouse and one the Kilpatrick boys say "that's for white chillum." They say "we ain't no niggers, 'cause we got the same daddy you has, and he comes to see us near every day and fotches us clothes and things from town." They is fussin' and missy Kilpatrick is listening; out her chamber window. She heard them white niggers say "he is our daddy and we call him daddy when he comes to our house to see our mama."

When massa come home that evenin' his wife hardly say nothin' to him, and he ask her what the matter and she tells him, "since you asks me, I'm studyin'; in my mind 'about them white young 'uns of that yaller nigger wench from Baton Rouge." He say "Now, honey, I fotches that gal jus for you 'cause she a fine seamster." She say, "it look kind of funny they got the same kind of hair and eyes ads my chillun and they got a nose looks like yours." He say, "Honey, you jus' payin' 'tention to talk of li'l chillun that ain't got no mind to what they say." She say, "Over in Mississippi I got a home and plenty with my daddy and I got that in my mind." Well, she didn't never leave and massa bough her a fine, new span of surrey hosses. But she don't ever have no more chillun and she ain't so cordial with the massa. Margaret, that yallow gal, has more white young 'uns, but they don't never go down the hill no more to the big house.

Aunt Chayney was jus' out of bed with a sucklin' baby one time, and she run away. Some say that was 'nother baby of massa's breedin'. She don't come to the house to nurse her baby, so they misses her and old Solomon gits the nigger hounds and takes her trail. They gits near her and she grabs a limb and tires to hist herself in a tree, but them dogs grab her and pull her down. The men hollers them onto her, and the dogs tore her naker and et the breasts plumb off her body. She got well and lived to be a old woman, but 'nother woman has to suck her baby and she ain't got no sign of breasts no more.

—Mary Reynolds in the WPA narratives online: *Texas Narratives, Vol. 4, Part 3*, 242–3. Library of Congress.

Honey, I don't like to talk 'bout dem times, 'cause my mother did suffer misery. You know der was an overseer who use to tie mother up ion de barn with a rope aroun' her arms up over her head, while she stood on a block. Soon as dey got her tied, dis block was moved an' her feet dangled, yo' know, couldn't tech de flo'. Dis ol man, now, would start beatin' her nekkid 'til de blood run down her back to her heels. I took an' seed th' whelps an' scars fer my own self wid dese two eyes. Was a whip like dey use to use on horses, it was a piece of leather 'bout as wide as my han' from little finger to thumb. After dey beat my mum all dey wanted another overseer. . . . Well honey dis man would bathe her in salt and water. Don't you kno' dem places wuz a hurtin'. . . . I asked mother "what she done fer 'em to beat and do her so?" She said, "nothin." Tother than she refused to be wife to dis man. And muma say if he didn't treat her dis way a dozen times, it wasn't nary one. Mind you, now muma's master didn't know dis wuz going on. You know, if slaves would tell, why dem overseers would kill 'em.

—Minnie Fulkes in the WPA narratives online: *Virginia Narratives, Vol. 16, Part 5*, 11. Library of Congress.

What I say am de facts. If I's one day old, I's way over 90, and I's born in Bell County, right here in Texas, and am owned by Massa William Black. He owns my mammy and pappy too. Massa Black has a big plantation but he has more niggers dan he need for work on dat place, 'cause he am a nigger trader. He buy and sell all de time. Massa Black am awful cruel and he whip de cullud folks and works 'em hard and feed dem poorly. . . . I has de correct mem'randum of when de war start. Massa Black sold we'uns right den. Mammy and pappy powerful glad to git sold, and dey and I is put on de block with 'bout ten other niggers. . . . One man shows intres' in pappy. His name Hawkins. He talk to pappy and pappy talk to him and say, "Dem my women and chiles. Please buy all of us and have mercy on we'uns." Massa Hawkins say, "Dat gal an a likely lookin' nigger, she am portly and strong, but three am more den I wants, I guess."

De sale start and befo' long pappy am put on de block. Massa Hawkins wins de bid for pappy and when mammy put on de block, he wins de bid for her. Den dere am three or four other niggers sold befo' my time comes. Den Massa Black calls me to de block an de auction man say, "What am I offer for dis portly, strong young wench. She never been 'bused and will make de good breeder." I wants to hear Massa Hawkins bid, but him say nothin'. Two other men am biddin' 'gainst each other and I sho' has de worryment. Dere am tears comin' down my cheeks 'cause I's bein' sold to some man dat would make sep'ation from my mammy. One man bids $500 and de auction man ask, "De I hear more? She am gwine at $500.00." Den someone say $525.00 an de auction man say "She am sold for $525.00 to Massa Hawkins." I am glad and 'cited! Why I's quiverin' all over.

Dere am one thing Massa Hawkins does to me what I can't shunt from my mind. I knows he don't do it fer meanness, but I allus holds it 'gainst him. What he done am force me to live with dat nigger, Rufus, 'gainst my wants. After I been at the place 'bout a year, de massa come to me and say, "You gwine live with Rufus in dat cabin over yonder. Go fix it for livin.'" I's 'bout sixteen year old and has no larnin', and I's jus' igno'mus chile. I's thought dat him mean to me to tend de cabin for Rufus and some other niggers. Well, dat am start de pestigation for me.

I's took charge of de cabin after work am done and fixes supper. Now, I don't like dat Rufus, 'cause he a bully. He am big and 'cause he so, he think everybody do what him say. We'uns has supper, den I goes here and dere talkin', 'till I's ready for sleep and den I gits in de bunk. After I's in, dat nigger some and crawl in de bunk with me 'fore I knews it. I says, "what you means, you fool nigger?" He say fer me to hush de mouth. "Dis am my bunk, too," he say.

"You's teched in de head. Git out," I's told him, and I puts de feet 'gainst him and give him a shove and out he go on de floor 'fore he knew what I's doin'. Dat nigger jump up and he mad. He look like de wild bear. He starts for de bunk and I jumps quick fer de poker. It am 'bout three feet long an when he comes at me I lets him have it over de head. Did dat nigger stop in he tracks? I's say he did. He looks at me steady for a minute and you's could tell he thinkin' hard. Den he go and set on de bench and say "Jus wait. You thinks it am smart, but you's am foolish in de head. Dey's gwine larn you somethin.'"

"Hush yous big mouth and stay 'way from dis nigger, dat all I wants," I say, and jus' sets and hold dat poker in de hand. He jus' sets, lookin' like de bull. Dere we'uns sets and sets for 'bout and hour and den he go out and I bars de door.

De nex' day I goes to de missy and tells he what Rufus wants and missy say dat am de massa's wishes. She say "Yous am de portly gal an Rufus am de portly man. De massa wants you'uns to bring forth portly chillen." I's thinkin' 'bout what de missy say, but say to myself, "I's not gwine live with dat Rufus." Dat night when him come in de cabin, I grabs de poker and sirs on de bench and says "Git 'way from me, nigger, 'fore I busts yous brains out and stomp on dem." He say nothin' and git out.

De nex' day de massa call me and tell me, "woman, I's pay big money for you and I's done dat for de cause I wants yous to raise me chillens. I's put yous to live with Rufus for dat purpose. Now, if you doesn't want whippin' at de stake, yous do what I wants."

I thinks 'bout massa buying' me effen de block and savin' me from bein' sep'rated from my folks, and 'bout bein' whipped at de stake. Dere it am. What am I's to do? So I 'cides to do as de massa wish and so I yields.

—Rose Williams in the WPA narratives online: *Texas Narratives, Vol. 16, Part 4*, 174–8. Library of Congress.

White Women: Kindness and Cruelty

Some enslaved women relied upon their white mistresses for help and advice, especially in matters concerning health and reproduction. Worried about their slaves' well-being, some mistresses, like Fanny Kemble, a British actress who married an American slaveholder before moving to his Georgia plantation, spent considerable time helping their female slaves. Kemble grew increasingly distressed about the mental and physical health of her female slaves, especially because her husband permitted them only a limited amount of respite after giving birth. In contrast, WPA respondent Ellen Campbell remembered the white woman to whom she was hired out lashing out toward her with violence. After the incident, Ellen's horrified mistress took her back into her own possession. Sarah Graves recalled a whipping she received from her "Ole Mistress" for a "crime" she never committed.

I have had several women at the house today asking for advice and help for their sick children: they all came from Number Two, as they call it, that is, the settlement or cluster of Negro huts nearest to the main one, where we may be said to reside. In the afternoon I went thither, and found a great many of the little children ailing: there had been an unusual mortality among them at this particular settlement this winter.

Yesterday evening I had a visit that made me very sorrowful, if anything connected with these poor people can be called more sorrowful than their whole condition; but Mr. [Butler]'s declaration, that he will receive no more statements of grievances or petitions for redress through me, makes me as desirous now as shunning the vain appeals of these unfortunates as I used to be of receiving and listening to them. The imploring cry: "Oh Missis!" that greets me whichever way I turn, makes me long to stop my ears now; for what can I say or do any more for them? The poor little favors—the rice, the sugar, the flannel—that they beg for with such eagerness, and receive with such exuberant gratitude, I can, it is true, supply, and words and looks of pity, and counsel of patience, and such instruction in womanly habits of decency and cleanliness as may enable them to better, in some degree, their own hard lot; but to thee entreaty: "Oh, missis, you speak to massa for us! Oh, missis, you beg massa for us!, Oh, missis, you tell massa for we, he sure do as you say!" I cannot now answer as formerly, and I turn away choking and with eyes full of tears from the poor creatures, not even daring to promise any more the faithful transmission of their prayers.

The women who visited me yesterday evening were all in the family way, and came to entreat of me to have the sentence (what else can I call it?) modified which condemns them to resume their labor of hoeing in the fields three weeks after their confinement. They knew, of course, that I can-not interfere with their appointed labor, and therefore their sole entreaty was that I would use my influence with Mr. [Butler] to obtain for them a month's respite from labor in the field after childbearing. Their principle spokeswoman, a woman with a bright sweet face, called Mary, and a very sweet voice, which is by no means an uncommon excellence among them, appealed to my own experience; and while she spoke of my babies, and my carefully tended, delicately nursed, and tenderly watched confinement and convalescence, and implored me to have a kind of labor given to them less exhausting during the month after their confinement, I held the table before me so hard in order not to cry that I think my fingers ought to have left a mark on it. At length I told them that Mr. [Butler] had forbidden me to bring him any more complaints from them, for that he thought the ease with which I received and believed their stories only tended to make them discontented, and that, therefore, I feared I could not promise to take their petitions to him; but that he would be coming down to "the point" soon, and that they had better come then sometime when I was with him, and say what they had just been saying to me; and with this, and various small bounties, I was forced, with a heavy heart, to dismiss them; and when they were gone, with many exclamations of: "Oh yes, missis, you will, you will speak to massa for we; God bless you, missis, we sure you will!" I had my cry out for them, for myself, for *us*. All these women had had large families, and *all* of them had lost half their children, and several of them had lost more.

—Frances Anne Kemble, *Journal of a Residence on a Georgian Plantation in 1838–1839, with an Intro-duction by John A. Scott* (Athens: University of Georgia Press, 1984 [1863]), 130, 222–3.

When I wus 'bout ten years old dey started me tottin' water—you know ca'in water to de hands in de field. 'Bout two years later I got my first field job, 'tending sheep. When I wus fifteen my old Missus gib me to Miss Eva—you know she de one marry Colonel Jones. My young missus was fixin' to git married, but she couldn't on account de war, so she brought me to town and rented me out to a lady runnin' a boarding house. De rent wus paid to my missus. One day I wus takin' a tray from de out-door kitchen to de house when I stumbled and dropped it. De food spill all over de ground. De lady go so mad she picked up a butcher knife and cop me in de haid. I went runnin' till I come to de place where my white folks live. Miss Eva took me and wash de blood out mah head and put medicine on it, and she wrote a note to de lady and she say, "Ellen is my slave, give to me by my mother. I wouldn't had dis happen to her no more dan to me. She won't come back dere not more."

—Ellen Campbell in the WPA narratives online: *Georgia Narratives, Vol. 4, Part 4*, 222. Library of Congress.

Yes'm. Some masters was good an' some was bad. My mama's master whipped his slaves for pastime. My master not so bad as some was to their slaves. I've had many a whippin', some I deserved, and some I got blamed for doin' things the master's children did. My master whipped his slaves with a cat-o-nine-tails. He's say to me, "You ain't had a curryin' down for some time. Come here!!!" Then he whipped me with the cat. The cat was made of nine strips of leather fastened onto the end of a whip. Lots of times when he hit me, the cat left nine strips of blood on my back. Yes ma'am.

I belong to the African Methodist Episcopal Church, an' I ain't never cussed but once in my life, an' that was one time I nearly got two whippin's for somethin' I didn't do. Some of master's kin folks had a weddin', an' we walked to the church, an' somebody kicked dust on the bride's clothes a' I got blamed but I ain't neber kicked it. The master's daughter, Puss, she kicked it. Ole mistress she whipped me. Yes'm she whipped me. It was the worst whip-pin' I ever got. The worst whippin' in my whole life, an' I still got the marks on my body. Yes'm. I got 'em yet.

When the master come home, he was goin' to whip me again, an' I got mad, an' told him it was a lie, an' if Puss said I kicked dust on the white folks she was a DAMNED LYIN' DEVIL. He took the switch an' gave Puss a whippin' for tellin' a lie. Yes'm. That's the only time I ever cussed in my life. Yes'm, an' that's about all I knows about slavery and folks ways hereabouts.

—Sarah Graves in the WPA narratives online: *Missouri Narratives, Vol. 10*, 131–3. Library of Congress.

Escape in Antebellum Times

Only occasionally did enslaved women flee alone, mostly because they did not want to leave their children behind. Harriet Jacobs hid in her free grandmother's loft space for several years before escaping North after running away from the clutches of her master, who sexually assaulted her. Here, she describes her joy at witnessing her children playing from her confined space. Similarly, Annie Burton's mother fled after a whipping and Annie did not see her for three years. But not all enslaved women who ran away wanted to escape their owners. Some women's immediate priority was to seek their loved ones. For example, Emanuel Elmore's mother was sold from the plantation where she had raised her children, but she escaped and eventually returned to her family in South Carolina. Ellen Craft fled slavery with her husband, William, famously disguised as a white gentleman, while her husband pretended to be her slave.

I bored three rows of holes, one above another; then I bored out the inter-stices between. I thus succeeded in making one hole about an inch long and

—Sarah Frances Shaw Graves, Age 87. *Born in Slavery: Slave Narratives from the Federal Writers' Project, 1936–1938*, Library of Congress.

an inch broad. I sat by it late into the night, to enjoy the little whiff of air that floated in. In the morning I watched for my children. The first person I saw in the street was Dr. Flint. I had a shuddering, superstitious feeling that it was a bad omen. Several familiar faces passed by. At last I heard the merry laugh of children, and presently two sweet little faces were looking up at me, as though they knew I were there, and were conscious of the joy they imparted. How I longed to *tell* them I was there!

—Harriet Jacobs, *Incidents in the Life of a Slave Girl* (New York: Dover, 2001 [1861]), 97.

My mistress often told me that my father was a planter who owned a plantation about two miles from ours. He was a white man, born in Liverpool, England. He died in Lewisville, Alabama, in the year 1875. I will venture to say that I only saw my father a dozen times, when I was about four years old; and those times I saw him only from a distance, as he was driving by the great house of our plantation. Whenever my mistress saw him going by, she would take me by the hand and run out upon the piazza, and exclaim, "Stop there, I say! Don't you want to see and speak to and caress your darling child? She often speaks of you and wants to embrace her dear father. See what a bright and beautiful daughter she is, a perfect picture of yourself. Well, I declare, you are an affectionate father." I well remember that whenever my mistress would speak thus and upbraid him, he would whip up his horse and get out of sight and hearing as quickly as possible. My mistress's action was, of course, intended to humble and shame my father. I never spoke to him, and cannot remember that he ever noticed me, or in any way acknowledged me to be his child.

My mother and my mistress were children together, and grew up to be mothers together. My mother was the cook in my mistress's household. One morning when master had gone to Eufaula, my mother and my mistress got into an argument, the consequence of which was that my mother was whipped, for the first time in her life. Whereupon, my mother refused to do any more work, and ran away from the plantation. For three years we did not see her again.

—Annie L. Burton, *Memories of Childhood's Slavery Days* (Boston: Ross Brown Publishing Company, 1909), 7–8. *Documenting the American South*, The University of North Carolina at Chapel Hill Library, http://docsouth.unc.edu/fpn/burton/menu.html.

Pa . . . married Dorcas Cooper [Elmore's mother], who belonged to the Coopers at Staunton Military Academy. When pa left Alabama to refugee back, he had to leave Dorcas. They did not love their marster anyway. He put Dorcas up on the block with a red handkerchief around her head and gave her a red apple to eat. She was sold to a man whose name I have forgotten. When they herded them she got away and was months making her way back to South Carolina. Those Africans sure were strong. She said that she stayed in the woods at night. Negroes along the way would give her bread and she would kill rabbits and squirrels and cook and eat in the woods. . . . When she did get back to Col. Elmore's place, she was lanky, ragged and poor, but Col. Elmore was glad to see her and told her he was not going to let anybody take her off. Jenny [Elmore's father's new wife] had cared so well for her children while she was off, that she liked her. They lived in the same house with Pa

Frontispiece image from Annie L. Burton, *Memories of Childhood's Slavery Days* (Boston: Ross Brown Publishing Company, 1909). *Documenting the American South*, The University of North Carolina at Chapel Hill Library, http://docsouth.unc.edu/fpn/burton/frontis.html.

till my mother died. . . . One time a lot of the negroes in the quarter got drunk and ma got to fighting all of them. When she got sobered up she was afraid that Col. Elmore was going to send her back to Alabama; so she went and hid in the woods. Pa took food to her. In about a month Col. Elmore asked where she was, and pa just looked sheepish and grinned. Col. Elmore told pa to go and bring her back, for he said he was tired of having his rations carried to the woods; so ma came hime. She has stayed off three months. She never felt well anymore, and she died in about three more months. Pa and Jenny kept us till we got big and went off for ourselves.

—Emanuel Elmore in the WPA narratives online: *South Carolina Narratives, Vol. 14, Part 2,* 8–10. Library of Congress.

The greatest excitement prevails at a slave-hunt. The slaveholders and their hired ruffians appear to take more pleasure in this inhuman pursuit than English sportsmen do in chasing a fox or a stag. Therefore, knowing what we should have been compelled to suffer, if caught and taken back, we were more than anxious to hit upon a plan that would lead us safely to a land of liberty. But, after puzzling our brains for years, we were reluctantly driven to the sad conclusion that it was almost impossible to escape from slavery in Georgia, and travel 1,000 miles across the slave States. We therefore resolved to get the consent of our owners, be married, settle down in slavery, and en-deavour to make ourselves as comfortable as possible under that system; but at the same time ever to keep our dim eyes steadily fixed upon the glimmer-ing hope of liberty, and earnestly pray God mercifully to assist us to escape from our unjust thralldom. We were married, and prayed and toiled on till December, 1848, at which time (as I have stated) a plan suggested itself that proved quite successful, and in eight days after it was first thought of we were free from the horrible trammels of slavery, and glorifying God who had brought us safely out of a land of bondage.

Knowing that slaveholders have the privilege of taking their slaves to any part of the country they think proper, it occurred to me that, as my wife was nearly white, I might get her to disguise herself as an invalid gentleman, and assume to be my master, while I could attend as his slave, and in that manner we might effect our escape. After I thought of the plan, I suggested it to my wife, but at first she shrank from the idea. She thought it was almost impos-sible for her to assume that disguise, and travel a distance of 1,000 miles across the slave States. However, on the other hand, she also thought of her condition. She saw that the laws under which we lived did not recognize her to be a woman, but a mere chattel, to be bought and sold, or otherwise dealt with as her owner might see fit. Therefore the more she contemplated her helpless condition, the more anxious she was to escape from it. So she said, "I think it is almost too much for us to undertake; however, I feel that God is on our side, and with his assistance, notwithstanding all the difficulties, we shall be able to succeed. Therefore, if you will purchase the disguise, I will try to carry out the plan."

But after I concluded to purchase the disguise, I was afraid to go to any one to ask him to sell me the articles. It is unlawful in Georgia for a white man to trade with slaves without the master's consent. But, notwithstanding this, many persons will sell a slave any article that he can get the money to buy. Not that they sympathize with the slave, but merely because his testimony is not admitted in court against a free white person. Therefore, with little difficulty I went to different parts of the town, at odd times, and purchased things piece by piece, (except the trowsers which she found necessary to make,) and took them home to the house where my wife resided. She being a ladies' maid, and a favourite slave in the family, was allowed a little room to herself; and amongst other pieces of furniture which I had made in my overtime, was a chest of drawers; so when I took the articles home, she locked them up carefully in these drawers. No one about the premises knew that she had anything of the kind.

—William Craft, *Running a Thousand Miles for Freedom; or, the Escape of William and Ellen Craft from Slavery* (London: William Tweedie, 1860), 28–31. *Documenting the American South*, The University of North Carolina at Chapel Hill Library, http://docsouth.unc.edu/neh/craft/menu.html.

Memories of the Civil War and Union Troops

Female WPA respondents often recalled the arrival of Union troops in the South. For some, including Susan Matthews, this was a moment of great excitement because they hoped the Northern army would bring news of freedom. However, others, including Nellie Smith, remembered the Union soldiers in a much more negative light, as pillagers and thieves. Yet other young women remained confused by war and its consequences, and unsure about how it would affect them, as Kate Phoenix illustrates.

My ma an her chillen wuz the onliest slaves my marster and mistis had. My pa belonged to some mo white folks that lived 'bout five miles from us. . . . I wuz raised in my mistis' house. I slept in her room; slep' on the foot of her bed to keep her feets warm and everywhere my mistis went I went to. My marster and mistis wuz sho good to us an we loved 'em. My ma, she done the cooking and the washing fer the family and she could work in the fields jes lak a man. She could pick her three hundred pounds of cotton or pull as much fodder as any man. She wuz strong an she had a new baby mos' ev'y yeat. My marster and mistis liked for [her] to have a lot of chillen 'cause that helped ter make 'em richer.

Does I remember 'bout the Yankees coming? Yes ma'am I sho does. The white chillen an us had been looking for 'em and looking for 'em. We wanted 'em to come. We knowed 'twould be fun to see 'em. And sho 'nuf one day

I was out in de front yard to see and I seed a whole passal of men in blue coats coming down de road. I hollered "Here come de Yankees." I knowed twus dem an my mistis an my ma and ev'y body come out in the front yard to see 'em. The Yankees stopped an the leading man with the straps on his shoulders talked to us an de men got water outen de well. No'm, they didn't take nothing an they hurt nothing. After a while they jes went on down the road; they sho looked hot an dusty an tired. After de war wuz over my pas, he comed up to our house an got my ma an all us chillen an carried us down to his marster's place. I didn't want to go cause I loved my mistis an she cried when we left. My pa's ole marster let him have some land to work on shares.

—Susan Matthews in the WPA narratives online: *Georgia Narratives, Vol. 4, Part 3*, 116–7. Library of Congress.

It wasn't long after the war [began] when the Yankees come to Athens. Folks had to bury or hide everything they could for them Yankees jus' took anything they could git their hands on, 'specially good food. They would catch up other folks' chickens and take hams from the smokehouses, and they jus' laughed in folks' faces if they said anything 'bout it. They camped in the woods here on Hancock Avenue, but of course it wasn't settled then lak it is now. I was mighty scared of them Yankees and they didn't lak me neither. One of 'em called me a little white-headed devil.

One of my aunts worked for a northern lady that they called Mrs. Meeker, who lived where the old Barrow home is now. Evvy summer when she went back up North she would leave my aunt and uncle to take care of her place. It was right close to the Yankee's camp, and the soldiers made my aunt cook for them sometimes. I was livin' with her then, and I was so scared of 'em that I stayed right by her side as long as the Yankees was hangin' 'round Athens.

—Nellie Smith in the WPA narratives online: *Georgia Narratives, Vol. 4, Part 3*, 309–10. Library of Congress.

When de war broke out I didn't know what it was for. Mrs. Harris had three sons that was living some place away, and they went to war. Mrs. Harris was hatin' the North and I was hatin' the North too. I thought the North was kind of like a spider in a dream that was going to come and wipe away de house and carry me off. When I heard 'bout Santa Clause that was goin' to come down de chimney, I screamed. I gits a poker and wasn't goin' to let him in. Everythin' was like a tangled dream jus' opposite to what I found out later it was. I believes now Mrs. Harris liked to get me thinkin' weren't like they was. . . . I 'members when the end of the war came. Mrs. Harris set up a cryin'. I cried harder than she does. I didn't know what worser was to befall, but I thinks it was dangerous to breathe. Then I hears some slaves shoutin' glad cose they was free. I didn't know what "free" meant and I askes Mrs. Harris if I was free. She says I was free but was goin' to repent of it. But she told me she wasn't going to whip me anymore; and she never did, cose my father came and took me away.

—WPA respondent Kate Phoenix in *The American Slave: A Composite Autobiography, Supplement Series 2: Texas Narratives, Vol. 8, Part 7* (Westport, CT: Greenwood Press, 1979), 3082–6.

Enslaved Women's Changing Relationships with Their Owners

Enslaved women's relationships with white owners changed during the Civil War. White mistresses in particular grew increasingly fearful of what their future might hold. Mattie Jackson's mistress vented her rage upon Mattie, while Ann Valentine described her mistreatment at the hands of her owners in a letter to her husband. Annie Burton remembered her owners discussing what might happen to their slaves if the Confederacy lost the war. She also noted, with a keen sense of irony, how the arrival of Yankee troops led white masters and mistresses—rather than slaves—to run away from their homes. Plantation mistress Keziah Goodwyn Hopkins Brevard displays typically racist attitudes toward enslaved women in her Civil War diary, seeing her female slaves as both "unprepared" for freedom and innately promiscuous.

Soon after the war commenced the rebel soldiers encamped near Mr. Lewis' residence, and remained there one week. They were then ordered by General Lyons to surrender, but they refused. There were seven thousand Union and seven hundred rebel soldiers. The Union soldiers surrounded the camp and took them and exhibited them through the city and then confined them in prison. I told my mistress that the Union soldiers were coming to take the camp. She replied that it was false, that it was General Kelly coming to re-enforce Gen. Frost. In a few moments the alarm was heard. I told Mrs. L. the Unionists had fired upon the rebels. She replied it was only the salute of Gen. Kelley. At night her husband came home with the news that Camp Jackson was taken and all the soldiers prisoners.

Mrs. Lewis asked how the Union soldiers could take seven hundred men when they only numbered the same. Mrs. L replied they had seven thousand. She was much astonished, and cast her eye around to us for fear we might hear her. Her suspicion was correct; there was not a word passed that escaped our listening ears. My mother and myself could read enough to make out the news in the papers. The Union soldiers took much delight in tossing a paper over the fence to us. It aggravated my mistress very much. . . . The days of sadness for mistress were days of joy for us. We shouted and laughed to the top of our voices. My mistress was more enraged than ever—nothing pleased her. One evening, after I had attended to my usual duties, and I supposed all was complete, she, in a terrible rage, declared I should be punished at night. I did not know the cause, neither did she. She went immediately and selected a switch. She placed it in the corner of the room to await the return of her husband at night to whip me. As I was not pleased with the idea of a whipping I bend the switch in the shape of a W, which was the first letter of his name, and after I had attended to the dining room my fellow servant and myself walked away and stopped with an aunt of mine during the night. In the morning we made our way to the Arsenal, but could gain no admission. While we were wandering about seeking protection, the girl's father overtook us and persuaded us to return home. We finally complied. All was quiet. Not a word was spoken respecting our sudden departure. All went on as usual. I was permitted to attend to my work without interruption until three weeks later. One morning I entered Mrs. Lewis' room, and she was in a room adjoining, complaining of something I had neglected. Mr. L. then enquired if I had done my work. I told him I had. She then flew into a rage and told him I was saucy, and to strike me, and he immediately gave me a severe blow with a stick of wood, which inflicted a deep wound upon my head. The blood ran over my clothing, which gave me a frightful appearance.

Mr. Lewis then ordered me to change my clothing immediately. As I did not obey be became more enraged, and pulled me into another room and threw me on the floor, placed his knee on my stomach, slapped me on the face and beat me with his fist, and would have punished me more had not my mother interfered. He then told her to go away or he would compel her to, but she remained until he left me. I struggled mightily, and stood him a good test for a while, but he was fast conquering me when my mother came. He was aware my mother could usually defend herself against one man, and both of us would overpower him, so after giving his wife strict orders to take me up stairs and keep me there, he took his carriage and drove away. But she forgot it, as usual. She was highly gratified with my appropriate treatment, as she called it, and retired to her room, leaving me to myself. I then went to my mother and told her I was going away. She bid me go, and added "May the Lord help you."

—Mattie J. Jackson, *The Story of Mattie J. Jackson: Her Parentage, Experience of Eighteen Years in Slavery, Incidents during the War, Her Escape from Slavery: A True Story* (Lawrence [MA]: Sentinel Office, 1866), 6–12. *Documenting the American South*, The University of North Carolina at Chapel Hill Library, http://docsouth.unc.edu/neh/jacksonm/menu.html.

My dear husband, you do not know how badly I am treated. They [her own-ers] are treating me worse every day. Our child cries for you. Send me some money as soon as you can for me and my child are almost naked. . . . Do the best you can and do not fret too much for me for it won't be long before I will be free and then all we make will be ours. Your affectionate wife.

—Letter from "Ann" to her husband, Andrew Valentine, of the 2nd Missouri Colored Infantry. Quoted in Ella Forbes, *African American Women during the Civil War* (New York and London: Gar-land, 1998), 189.

Young as I was then, I remember this conversation between master and mis-tress, on master's return from the gate one day, when he had received the latest news: "William, what is the news from the seat of war?" "A great battle was fought at Bull Run, and the Confederates won," he replied. "Oh, good, good," said mistress, "and what did Jeff Davis say?" "Look out for the blockage. I do not know what the end may be soon," he answered. "What does Jeff Davis mean by that?" she asked. "Sarah Anne, I don't know unless he means that the niggers will be free." "O, my God, what shall we do?" "I presume," he said, "we shall have to put our boys to work and hire help." "But," she said, "what will the niggers do if they are free? Why, they will starve if we don't keep them." "Oh well," he said, "let them wander, if they will not stay with their owners. I don't doubt that many owners have been good to their slaves, and they would rather remain with their owners than wander about without home or country."

One day master heard that the Yankees were coming our way, and he immediately made preparations to get his goods and valuables out of their reach. The big six-mule team was brought to the smoke-house door, and loaded with hams and provisions. After being loaded, the team was put in the care of two of the most trustworthy and valuable slaves that my master owned, and driven away. It was master's intention to have these things taken to a swamp, and there concealed in a pit that had recently been made for the purpose. But just before the team left the main road for the by-road that led to the swamp, the two slaves were surprised by the Yankees, who at once took possession of the provisions, and started the team toward Clayton, where the Yankees had headquarters. The road to Clayton ran past our plantation. One of the slave children happened to look up the road, and saw the Yankees coming, and gave warning. Whereupon, my master left unceremoniously for the woods, and remained concealed there for five days. The niggers had run away whenever they got a chance, but now it was master's and the other white folks' turn to run.

The Yankees rode up to the piazza of the great house and inquired who owned the plantation. They gave orders that nothing must be touched or taken away, as they intended to return shortly and take possession. My mistress and the slaves watched for their return day and night for more than a week, but the Yankees did not come back.

One morning in April, 1865, my master got the news that the Yankees had left Mobile Bay and crossed the Confederate lines, and that the Emancipation Proclamation had been signed by President Lincoln. Mistress suggested that the slaves should not be told of their freedom; but master said he would tell them, because they would soon find it out, even if he did not tell them. Mistress, however, said she could keep my mother's three children, for my mother had now been gone so long.

All the slaves left the plantation upon the news of their freedom, except those who were feeble or sickly. With the help of these, the crops were gathered. My mistress and her daughters had to go to the kitchen and to the washtub. My little half-brother, Henry, and myself had to gather chips, and help all we could. My sister, Caroline, who was twelve years old, could help in the kitchen. After the war, the Yankees took all the good mules and horses from the plantation, and left their old army stock. We children chanced to come across one of the Yankees' old horses, that had "U. S." branded on him. We called him "Old Yank" and got him fattened up.

—Annie L. Burton, *Memories of Childhood's Slavery Days* (Boston: Ross Brown Publishing Company, 1909), 6–10. *Documenting the American South*, The University of North Carolina at Chapel Hill Library, http://docsouth.unc.edu/fpn/burton/menu.html.

They are not prepared for freedom, many of them set no higher value on themselves than the beasts of the field do. I know a family in five miles of me where there are six women who have and have had children for thirty years back and not one of them but [have] been bastards and only one ever had a husband. . . . I own many slaves and many of the females are of the lowest cast—making miserable their own fellow servants by meddling with the husbands of others—I am not excusing the males, but in the world they are not so degraded by such conduct as the females.

—John Hammond Moore (ed.), *A Plantation Mistress on the Eve of the Civil War: The Diary of Keziah Goodwyn Hopkins Brevard, 1860–1861* (Columbia: University of South Carolina Press, 1993), 39.

Enslaved Women's Experiences in Civil War Camps

Some enslaved women lived and worked in Union army camps during the Civil War. Francis Johnson fled to a Kentucky camp after being mistreated by her master's son and because her husband had joined the Union army, as she explained in an affidavit to camp officials. Susie King Taylor ran away from her quarters in Georgia aged just thirteen to join other "contraband" slaves on St. Simon's Island, Georgia, where, like many other black women, she worked as a laundress before publishing her memoirs.

I am the wife of Nathan Johnson a soldier in Company F, 116th US Colored Infantry. I have three children and with them I belonged to Matthias Outon, Fayette County, Kentucky. My husband who belonged to Mary Outon, Woodford County, Kentucky, enlisted in the United States service at Camp Nelson in May 1864. . . . The day after my husband enlisted my master knew it and said that he (my husband) and all the "niggers" did mighty wrong in joining the army. . . . On Wednesday, March 8th 1865 my master's soon, Thomas Outon whipped me severely on my refusing to do some work which I was not in a position to perform. He beat me in the presence of his father who told him (Thomas Outon) to "buck me and give me a thousand" meaning thereby a thousand lashes. While beating me he threw me on the floor and as I was in this prostate and helpless condition he continued to whip me endeavoring at one time to tie my hands and at another time to make an indecent exposure of my person before those present.

—Francis Johnson, Affidavit submitted at Camp Nelson, Kentucky, 1865. Quoted in Ella Forbes, *African American Women during the Civil War* (New York and London: Garland, 1998), 177.

There were about six hundred men, women and children on St. Simon's, the women and children being in the majority, and we were afraid to go very far from our quarters in the daytime, and at night even to go out of the house for a long time, although the men were on the watch all the time; for there were not many soldiers on the island, only the marines who were on the gunboats along the coast. The rebels, knowing this, could steal by them undercover of the night, and getting on the island would capture any persons venturing out along and carry them to the mainland. Several of the men disappeared, and as they were never heard from we came to the conclusion they had been carried off in this way. . . . The first colored troops did not receive any pay for eighteen months, and the men had to depend wholly on what they received from the commissary, established by General Saxton. A great many of these men had large families, and as they had no money to support them, their wives were obliged to support themselves and children by washing for the officers of the gunboats and the soldiers, and making cakes and pies which they sold to the boys in camp.

—Susie King Taylor, *Reminiscences of My Life in Camp: An African American Woman's Civil War Memoir* (Athens and London: University of Georgia Press, 2006 [1902]), 14–16.

Memories of Emancipation

Many women interviewed by the WPA recalled the moment they learned they were free. Some heard about their emancipation from government officials, while at other times former masters told their slaves that they were now free. Yet other masters, including Tempie Cummins's owner, tried to hide news of freedom from their former slaves, or attempted to force them to remain in their quarters. While the immediate aftermath of emancipation brought great joy to formerly enslaved women, as Charlotte Brown conveys, the practical realities of trying to make a living often meant newly freed women had to maintain their onerous workloads even after slavery ended, as Harriet Robinson recalled.

De news come on a Thursday, an' all de slaves been shoutin' an' carryin' on till ev'rybody was tired out. 'member de fust Sunday of freedom. We was all sittin' roun' restin' an' tryin' to think what freedom meant an' ev'rybody was quiet an' peaceful. All at once ole Sister Carrie who was near 'bout a hundred started in to talkin':

> "Tain't no mo' sellin' today,
> Tain't no mo'hirn' today,
> Tain't no pullin' off shirts today,
> Its stomp down freedom today.
> Stomp it down!"

> An' when she says, "Stomp it down,"
>   all de slaves commence to shoutin' wid her:

> "Stomp down Freedom today—
> Stomp it down!
> Stomp down Freedom today!"

Wasn't no mo' peace day Sunday. Ev'rybody started in to sing an' shout once mo'. Fust thing you know dey done made up music to Sister Carrie's stomp song an' sang an' shouted dat song all de res' de day. Chile, dat was one glorious time!

—WPA respondent Charlotte Brown, in Charles L. Perdue, Robert E. Barden and Robert K. Phillips (eds.), *Weevils in the Wheat: Interviews with Virginia Ex-Slaves* (Charlottesville: University of Virginia Press, 1976), 58–59.

Young missy Betty like me and try larn me readin' and writin' and she slip to my room and have me doimn' right good. I larn the alphabet. But one day

Missy Jane cotch her schoolin' me and she say "Niggers don't need to know anything," and she lams me over the head with the butt of a cowhide whip. That white woman so rough, one day us makin' soap and some little chickens gits in the fire 'round the pot and he say I let 'em do it and make me walk barefoot though that bed of coals sev'ral times.

I heard 'bout freedom in September and they's pickin' cotton and a white man ride up to Master's house on a big white horse and the houseboy tell massa a man want to see him and he hollers "light, stranger." It was a gov'ment man, and he have the big book and a bunch papers and say why ain't massa turn the niggers loose. Massa say he tryin' git the crop out and he tell massa have the slaves in. Uncle Steven blows the cow horn what they used to call to eat and all the niggers come runnin' 'cause that horn mean, "come to the house, quick." That man reads the paper tellin' us we's free, but massa make us work sev'ral months after that. He say we git 20 acres land and a mule but we didn't git it.

Lots of niggers was kilt after freedom, 'cause the slaves in Harrison Country turn loose right at freedom and them in Rusk County wasn't. But they hears 'bout it and runs away to freedom in Harrison County and they owners have 'em bushwacked, that shot down. You could see lots of niggers hangin' to trees in Sabine bottom right after freedom, 'cause they catch 'em swimmin' cross Sabine Rive and shoot 'em. They sho' am goin' be lots of soul cry 'gainst 'em in Judgement!

—Susan Merritt in the WPA narratives online: *Texas Narratives, Vol. 16, Part 3*, 78. Library of Congress.

I never seed my grandparents 'cause my mother she sold in Alabama when she's 17 and they brung her to Texas and treat her rough. At mealtime they hand me a piece of cornbread and tell me "run 'long." Sometime I git little piece of meat and biscuit, 'bout once a month. I gathered up scraps the white chillun lef'. Marster was rough. He take two beech switches and twist them together and whip 'em to a stub. Many's the time I's bled from them whippin's. Our old mistus, she try to be good to us, I reckon, but she wus terribly lazy. She had two of us to wait on her and she didn' treat us good.

The white chillun tries teach me to read and write but I didn' larn much, 'cause I allus workin'. Mother was workin' in de house and she cooked too. She say she used to hide un the chimney corner and listen to what the white folks say. When freedom was 'clared, master wouldn' tell 'em, but mother she hear him tellin' mistus that the slaves was free but they didn't know it and he's not gwineter tell 'em till he makes another crop or two. When mother hear that she say she slip out the chimney corner and crack her heels together four times and shouts, "I'se free, I'se free." Then she runs to the field, 'gainst marster's will and tol' all the other slaves and they quit work. Then she run away and in the night she slip into a big ravine near the house and have them bring me to her. Master, he come out with his gun and shot at mother but she run down the ravine and gits away with me.

—Tempie Cummins in the WPA narratives online: *Texas Narratives, Vol. 16, Part 1*, 263–4. Library of Congress.

Tempie Cummins, ex-slave, Jasper, *Born in Slavery: Slave Narratives from the Federal Writers' Project, 1936–1938*, Library of Congress.

Women broke in mules throwed 'em and roped 'em. They's do it better'n men. . . . This was 'way back yonder in slavery, before the war. Whenever white folks had a baby born all de old niggers had to come thro the room and the master would be over 'hind the bed and he'd say, "Here's a new little mistress or master you got to work for." You had to say, "Yessuh Master" and bow real low or the overseer would crack you. Them was slavery days, dog days.

Master Sam didn't never whip me, but Miss Julia whipped me every day in the mawning. During the war she beat us so terrible. She say, "Your master's out fighting and losing blood trying to save you from them Yankees, so you kin git your'n here." Miss Julia would take me by my ears and butt my head against the wall. . . . I 'member the battle being fit. The white folks hurles all the jewelry and silver and all the gold in the Blue Ridge Mountains, in Orange, Texas. Master made all us niggers come together and git ready to leave 'cause the Yankees was coming. We took a steamer. Now this was in slavery time, sho' 'nuff slavery. Then we got on a steamship and pulled out to Galveston. Then he told the captain to feed we niggers. We was on the bay, not the ocean. We left Galveston and went on trains for Houston.

After the War, Master Colonel Sims went to git the mail and so he call Daniel Ivory, the overseer, and say to him "Go round to all the quarters and tall all the niggers to come up, I got a paper to read to 'em. They're free now, so you kin git you another job, 'cause I ain't got no more niggers which is my own." Niggers come up from the cabins nappy-headed, jest lak they gwine to the field. Master Colonel Sims say, "Carline (that's my mammy), you is free as me. Pa said bring you back and I'se gwina do jest that. So you go on and work and I'll pay you and your three oldest chillun $10.00 a month a head and $4.00 fer Harriet," that's me, and then he turned to the rest and say "Now all you'uns will receive $10.00 a head till the crops is laid by." Don't you know before he got half way throo', over half them niggers was gone.

—Harriet Robinson in the WPA narratives online: *Oklahoma Narratives, Vol. 13*, 271–3. Library of Congress.

After Slavery

Even as many women's everyday lives remained difficult after slavery, some women, such as Lucy Skipwith, used freedom's opportunities to escape from difficult relationships with their spouses. They linked freedom in a general sense with the opportunity to pursue their personal freedom. Women also desired to learn and to teach others, and some women, including Lucy Skipwith, set up schools on former plantations or in black churches. Northern black women often supported these educational initiatives and traveled to the South to set up and work in schools, including Louisa Jacobs, Harriet Jacobs's daughter, who worked in a Savannah school. Jacobs also comments on the newfound confidence of formerly enslaved women.

Hopewell, [Alabama,] December 7 1865

My dear Master:

I Received your letter a few days ago. I was truly glad to see that you were still alive & not gone the way to all the Earth. I was sorry that I had to part with Armistead but I have lived a life of trouble with him, & a white man has ever had to Judge between us, & now to be turned loose from under a master, I know that I could not live with him in no peace, therefore I left him. If you have any hard feelings against me on the subject, I hope that you will forgive me for Jesus sake.

I have a great desire to come to Va. to see you & my relations there & I hope that I may be able some day to do so. I have looked over my mind in regard to going to Liberia but I cannot get my consent to go there, but I thank you for your advice. None of our people are willing to go. I am still carrying on my School on the plantation & the Children are learning very fast. I have been thinking of putting up a large School next year as I can do more at that than I can at anything else, & I can get more children than I can teach.

—Letter from Lucy Skipwith to her master, quoted in Dorothy Sterling (ed.), *We Are Your Sisters: Black Women in the Nineteenth Century* (New York and London: W. W. Norton, 1984, 1997), 310.

I wish you could look upon my school of one hundred and thirty scholars. There are bright faces among them bent over puzzling books. . . . I have called mine the Lincoln School. We learn from the record kept at the Freedmen's Bureau, that there are two thousand two hundred children here. Some six or seven hundred are yet out of school. The freedman are interested in the education of their children. You will find a few who have to learn and appreciate what will be its advantage to them and theirs. The old spirit of the system, "I am the master and you are the slave" is not dead in Georgia. For instance, the people who live next door owned slaves. They are as poor as that renowned church mouse, yet they must have their servant. Employer and employee can never agree: the consequence is a new servant each week. The last comer had the look and air of one not easily crushed by circumstances. In the course of a few days, the neighbors were attracted to their doors by the loud voice of the would-be slaveholders. Out in the yard stood the mistress and her woman. The former had struck the latter. . . . as I looked at the black woman's fiery eye, her quivering form, and heard her dare her assailant to strike again, I was proud of her metal. In a short time the husband of the white woman made his appearance, and was about to deal a second blow, when she drew back, telling him she was no man's slave; that she was as free as he, and would take the law upon his wife for striking her. He blustered, but there he stood deprived of his old power to kill her if it had so pleased him. He ordered her to leave his premises immediately, telling her he should not pay her a cent for the time she had been with them. She quietly replied that she would see about that. She went to the Bureau, and very soon had things made right. . . . There are eight freedmen's schools here [Savannah, Georgia]; the largest has three hundred Scholars. The teachers of the two largest schools are colored, most of them natives of this place. These schools have been partially supported by the colored people, and will hereafter be entirely so.

—Louisa Jacobs, report about her and her mother's work with freedpeople in Savannah, Georgia. *The Freedmen's Record*, 1866, 55–56. *Documenting the American South*, The University of North Carolina at Chapel Hill Library, http://docsouth.unc.edu/fpn/jacobs/support14.html.

~

Bibliographic Essay

Inspired by the civil rights and the feminist movement, the history of enslaved women has attracted growing scholarly attention since the 1970s. Black Power activist Angela Y. Davis pioneered the writing of enslaved women's history with the publication of "Reflections on the Black Woman's Role in the Community of Slaves," in *The Black Scholar* 3, 4 (1971), 2–15. She later developed the article into the first chapter of her book *Women, Race, and Class* (New York: Random House, 1981), which stressed the "triple exploitation" of enslaved women as blacks, slaves, and women. Other scholars soon followed Davis's lead and started to explore various aspects of enslaved women's experiences during the international slave trade, the colonial period, the American Revolution, the antebellum era, the Civil War, and the postemancipation years.

Among the most useful general studies tracing the history of enslaved women are Darlene Clark Hine (ed.), *Black Women in American History: From Colonial Times throughout the Nineteenth Century*, 4 vols. (New York: Carlson, 1990); Rosalyn Terborg-Penn and Andrea Benton Rushing (eds.), *Women in Africa and the African Diaspora: A Reader* (Washington, DC: Howard University Press, 1987, 1996); David Barry Gaspar and Darlene Clark Hine (eds.), *More Than Chattel: Black Women and Slavery in the Americas* (Bloomington and Indianapolis: Indiana University Press, 1996); and Darlene Clark Hine and Kathleen Thompson (eds.), *A Shining Thread of Hope: The History of Black Women in America* (New York: Broadway Books, 1998). A convenient reference source is Daina Ramey Berry (ed.), *Enslaved Women in America: An Encyclopedia* (Westport, CT: Greenwood Press, 2012).

Studies examining gender in the context of the international slave trade include Herbert S. Klein, "African Women in the Atlantic Slave Trade," in Claire C. Robertson and Martin A. Klein (eds.), *Women and Slavery in Africa* (Madison: University of Wisconsin Press, 1983, 1997), 29–38, and David Eltis and Stanley L. Engerman's "Was the Slave Trade Dominated by Men?" *Journal of Interdisciplinary History* 23 (1992), 237–57 and "Fluctuations in Sex and Age Ratios in the Transatlantic Slave Trade, 1663–1864," in *Economic History Review* 46 (1993), 308–23.

A small, but growing body of scholarship focuses on enslaved women in colonial times and during the revolutionary era, including Joan R. Gundersen, "The Double Bonds of Race and Sex: Black and White Women in a Colonial Virginia Parish," *Journal of Southern History* 52 (1986), 351–72; Kathleen M. Brown's *Good Wives, Nasty Wenches, and Anxious Patriarchs: Gender, Race, and Power in Colonial Virginia* (Chapel Hill and London: University of North Carolina Press, 1996); Kirsten Fischer, *Suspect Relations: Sex, Race, and Resistance in Colonial North Carolina* (Ithaca: Cornell University Press, 2001); Jennifer Morgan, *Laboring Women: Reproduction and Gender in New World Slavery* (Philadelphia: University of Pennsylvania Press, 2004); Sharon Block, *Rape and Sexual Power in Early America* (Chapel Hill and London: University of North Carolina Press, 2006); and Jennifer M. Spear, *Race, Sex, and Social Order in Early New Orleans* (Baltimore: The Johns Hopkins University Press, 2009). A lack of sources by and about enslaved women means scholars have largely neglected to explore the role black women played in the Northern colonies, the American Revolution, and the early Republic.

Not surprisingly, the role of black women in the antebellum South has received considerable scholarly attention. Initially, many of the studies focused on exploring the interaction between white and black women, particularly emphasizing how white mistresses treated their female slaves. Studies concentrating on this aspect of antebellum slavery include Catherine Clinton's *The Plantation Mistress: Woman's World in the Old South* (New York: Pantheon, 1982); Elizabeth Fox-Genovese's *Within the Plantation Household: Black and White Women of the Old South* (Chapel Hill and London: University of North Carolina Press, 1988); Minrose C. Gwin's "Green-Eyed Monsters of the Slavocracy: Jealous Mistresses in Two Slave Narratives" in Darlene Clark Hine (ed.), *Black Women in American History: From Colonial Times through the Nineteenth Century, Vol. 2* (New York: Carlson, 1990), 559–72; Sally G. McMillen, *Southern Women: Black and White in the Old South* (Arlington Heights, IL: Harlan-Davidson, 1992, 2002); and Marli F. Weiner's *Mistresses and Slaves: Plantation Women in South Carolina 1830–1880* (Urbana and Chicago: University of Illinois Press, 1998). White mistresses' perspectives on enslaved women can also be found in Frances Anne Kemble's *Journal of a Residence on a Georgian Plantation in 1838–1839, with an Introduction by John A. Scott* (Athens: University of Georgia Press, 1984 [1863]) and Mary Boykin Chesnut's *Mary Chesnut's Diary with an Introduction by Catherine Clinton* (New York: Penguin Books, 2011). A significant departure from the focus on white mistresses was the publication of Deborah Gray White's *Ar'n't I a Woman?: Female Slaves in the Plantation South* (New York: W. W. Norton, 1985). White's book was the first monograph that focused on the experience of the women who lived in the slave quarters rather than emphasizing their interaction with whites.

Important works tracing the impact of the Civil War and emancipation on enslaved women include Jacqueline Jones, *Labor of Love, Labor of Sorrow: Black Women, Work and the Family from Slavery to the Present* (New York: Basic Books, 1985); Leslie Schwalm, *A Hard Fight for We: Women's Transition from Slavery to Freedom in South Carolina* (Urbana and Chicago: University of Illinois Press, 1997); Tera W. Hunter, *To 'Joy My Freedom: Southern Black Women's Lives and Labors after the Civil War* (Cambridge, MA and London: Harvard University Press, 1997); Rebecca J. Scott, *Degrees of Freedom: Louisiana and Cuba after Slavery* (Cambridge, MA and London: Belknap Press, 2005); Susan Eva O'Donovan, *Becoming Free in the Cotton South* (Cambridge, MA: Harvard University Press, 2007); Thavolia Glymph, *Out of the House of Bondage: The Transformation of the Plantation Household* (New York and Cambridge: Cambridge University Press, 2008); and Jim Downs, *Sick from Freedom: African American Illness and Suffering during the Civil War and Reconstruction* (New York: Oxford University Press, 2012).

While some scholars have taken a chronological approach to the study of female slaves, many more have pursued specific themes or topics. Enslaved families have been of obvious interest to historians studying female slavery. For an early example, see Kenneth Stampp, *The Peculiar Institution* (New York: Knopf, 1956, 1961, 1975). Stampp argued that mothers dominated enslaved families, while men were emasculated by their bondage. John Blassingame later challenged these views in *The Slave Community: Plantation Life in the Antebellum South* (New York and Oxford: Oxford University Press, 1972, 1979). Herbert Gutman's *The Black Family in Slavery and Freedom, 1750–1925* (New York: Pantheon, 1976) also emphasized the strong role enslaved men played as husbands and fathers.

Yet other historians have examined the structure of slave families. Anne Patton Malone, in *Sweet Chariot: Slave Family and Household Structure in Nineteenth-Century Louisiana* (Chapel Hill and London: University of North Carolina Press, 1992), stresses the significance of female-headed households, while Brenda Stevenson's *Life in Black and White: Family and Community in the Slave South* (New York and Oxford: Oxford University Press, 1996) explores enslaved families in Virginia. Another useful study of black family structure is Wilma Dunaway's *The African American Family in Slavery and Emancipation* (Cambridge: Cambridge University Press, 2003). Emily West, in *Chains of Love: Slave Couples in Antebellum South Carolina* (Urbana and Chicago: University of Illinois Press, 2004), assesses the importance of cross-plantation marriages among enslaved families. See also Tess Chakkalakal, *Novel Bondage: Slavery, Marriage, and Freedom in Nineteenth Century America* (Urbana and Chicago: University of Illinois Press, 2012); Rebecca Fraser, *Courtship and Love among the Enslaved in North Carolina* (Jackson: University Press of Mississippi, 2007); and Anthony E. Kaye, *Joining Places: Slave Neighborhoods in the Old South* (Chapel Hill and London: University of North Carolina Press, 2007).

Recent scholarship has drawn attention to the fact that not all slave families lived on large cotton plantations. See, for example, Damian Alan Pargas, *The Quarters and the Fields: Slave Families in the Non-Cotton South* (Gainesville: University Press of Florida Press, 2010); Diane Mutti Burke, *On Slavery's Border: Missouri's Small-Slaveholding Households 1815–1865* (Athens and London: University of Georgia Press, 2010); and Calvin Schermerhorn, *Money over Mastery, Family over Freedom: Slavery in the Antebellum Upper South* (Baltimore: The Johns Hopkins University Press, 2011).

An important part of family life in the slave quarters involved the raising of children. On the role of motherhood and child rearing, see Wilma King's *Stolen Childhood: Slave Youth in Nineteenth-Century America* (Bloomington: Indiana University Press, 1995) and Stephanie J. Shaw, "Mothering under Slavery in the Antebellum South," in Evelyn Nakano Glenn, Grace Chang, and Linda Rennie Forcey (eds.), *Mothering: Ideology, Experience, and Agency* (New York: Routledge, 1994), 237–58. Marie Jenkins Schwartz explores the idea of typical "life cycles" of female slaves in *Born in Bondage: Growing up Enslaved in the Antebellum South* (Cambridge, MA and London: Harvard University Press, 2000).

While scholars have documented that slave families were crucial for the psychological and physical survival of the slaves, owners threatened their stability by selling family members to other plantations. An exemplary study of the domestic slave trade and its impact on enslaved families is Michael Tadman's *Speculators and Slaves: Masters, Traders and Slaves in the Old South* (Madison: University of Wisconsin Press, 1989, 1996). See also Walter Johnson, *Soul by Soul: Life inside the Antebellum Slave Market* (Cambridge, MA and London: Harvard University Press, 1999); Edward Baptist, "'Cuffy,' 'Fancy Maids,' and 'One-Eyed Men': Rape, Commodification, and the Domestic Slave Trade in the United States," *American Historical Review* 106, 5 (2001),

1619–50; and Steven Deyle, *Carry Me Back: The Domestic Slave Trade in American Life* (New York: Oxford University Press, 2005).

The sale of relatives often sparked slave resistance, particularly among enslaved women. A pioneering piece on slave resistance, which devotes much time and attention to enslaved women, is R. A. and A. H. Bauer's "Day to Day Resistance to Slavery," *Journal of Negro History* 27 (1942), 388–418. Other important works on enslaved women's resistance include Darlene Clark Hine, "Female Slave Resistance: The Economics of Sex," *Western Journal of Black Studies* 3 (1979), 123–7; Mary Ellison, "Resistance to Oppression: Black Women's Response to Slavery in the United States," in *Slavery and Abolition* 4 (1983), 56–63; Betty Wood, "Some Aspects of Female Resistance to Chattel Slavery in Low Country Georgia, 1736–1815," *Historical Journal* 30 (1987), 603–22; and Stephanie Camp, *Closer to Freedom: Enslaved Women and Everyday Resistance in the Plantation South* (Chapel Hill and London: University of North Carolina Press, 2004).

Key works exploring enslaved women's culture include Shane White and Graham White, "Slave Clothing and African-American Culture in the Eighteenth and Nineteenth Centuries," *Past and Present*, 148 (1995), 149–86; and Shane White and Graham White, "Slave Hair and African American Culture in the Eighteenth and Nineteenth Centuries," *Journal of Southern History* 61, 1 (1995), 45–76. See also Josephine Beoku-Betts, "'She Make Funny Flat Cake She Call Saraka': Gullah Women and Food Practices under Slavery" in Larry E. Hudson (ed.), *Working toward Freedom: Slave Society and Domestic Economy in the American South* (New York: University of Rochester Press, 1994), 211–31. Work cultures and enslaved women's labor are considered in Betty Wood's *Women's Work, Men's Work: The Informal Slave Economies of Lowcountry Georgia* (Athens and London: University of Georgia Press, 1995); and Daina Ramey Berry's *"Swing the Sickle for the Harvest Is Ripe": Gender and Slavery in Antebellum Georgia* (Chicago and London: University of Illinois Press, 2007).

Literature on the health of enslaved women includes Diana E. Axelsen, "Women as Victims of Medical Experimentation: J. Marion Sims' Surgery on Slave Women, 1845–1850," *Sage: A Scholarly Journal on Black Women*, 2 (Fall 1985), 1–13; Sally G. McMillen's *Motherhood in the Old South: Pregnancy, Childbirth and Infant Rearing* (Baton Rouge and London: Louisiana State University Press, 1989); Liese Perrin, "Resisting Reproduction: Reconsidering Slave Contraception in the Old South," *Journal of American Studies* 35, 2 (2001), 255–74; Marie Jenkins Schwartz, *Birthing a Slave: Motherhood and Medicine in the Antebellum South* (Cambridge, MA and London: Harvard University Press, 2006); and Sharla Fett, *Working Cures: Healing, Health and*

Power on Southern Slave Plantations (Chapel Hill and London: University of North Carolina Press, 2002).

The relationship between enslaved women and the law forms the focus of many works. Judith Kelleher Shafer has written extensively on enslaved women, sexual exploitation, and the law in Louisiana. See, for example, *Becoming Free, Remaining Free: Manumission and Enslavement in New Orleans, 1846–1862* (Baton Rouge: Louisiana State University Press, 2003). Laura Edwards also explores the relationship between enslaved women and the law in *The People and Their Peace: Legal Culture and the Transformation of Inequality in the Post-Revolutionary South* (Chapel Hill and London: University of North Carolina Press, 2009).

Autobiographies of enslaved women also provide significant insight into their experiences. See, for example, Harriet Jacobs, *Incidents in the Life of a Slave Girl* and Jean Fagan Yellin's biography *Harriet Jacobs: A Life* (New York: Basic Civitas, 2004). Other enslaved women's autobiographies are featured in William Andrews (ed.), *Six Women's Slave Narratives* (New York and Oxford: Oxford University Press, 1988). See also Susie King Taylor, *Reminiscences of My Life in Camp: An African American Woman's Civil War Memoir* (originally published in 1902, Athens and London: University of Georgia Press, 2006) and Melton A. McLaurin, *Celia, A Slave: A True Story* (New York: Avon Books, 1991). For the letters of Lucy Skipwith, see Randall M. Miller, *Dear Master: Letters of a Slave Family* (Athens: University of Georgia Press, 1990).

Works Progress Administration interviews with former slaves are equally important in documenting the female slave experience. See, for example, Ira Berlin (ed.), *Remembering Slavery: African Americans Talk about Their Personal Experiences of Slavery and Emancipation* (New York: The New Press, 1999). Secondary works that make extensive use of WPA testimony include William Dusinberre, *Strategies for Survival: Recollections of Bondage in Antebellum Virginia* (Charlottesville and London: University of Virginia Press, 2009). Dusinberre also devotes some time to enslaved women in his earlier book, *Them Dark Days: Slavery in the American Rice Swamps* (New York and Oxford: Oxford University Press, 1996).

Other collections of primary sources relating to enslaved women include John W. Blassingame, *Slave Testimony: Two Centuries of Letters, Speeches, Interviews, and Autobiographies* (Baton Rouge: Louisiana State University Press, 1977); Catherine M. Lewis and J. Richard Lewis (eds.), *Women and Slavery in America: A Documentary History* (Fayetteville: University of Arkansas Press, 2011); and Dorothy Sterling (ed.), *We Are Your Sisters: Black Women in the Nineteenth Century* (New York and London: W. W. Norton, 1984, 1997). Online anthologies of WPA evidence can be found via the Library of Congress's "Born in Slavery" project: http://memory.loc.gov/ammem/snhtml/snhome.html.

Index

~

About the Author

Emily West is associate professor in American history at the University of Reading, UK. She studied for her undergraduate degree and PhD at the University of Liverpool, where she developed her interests in slavery, gender, and the antebellum South. She also spent twelve months at the University of South Carolina as a doctoral research fellow. Emily has taught at the University of Liverpool, Liverpool Hope University, Newcastle University, and the University of Reading. She has published widely on slavery, especially on relationships between enslaved couples, enslaved family life, and women and slavery. Emily has also published on relationships between the enslaved and free people of color. A regular attendee at academic conferences in the United Kingdom and the United States, Emily has presented on her work in the United Kingdom, the United States, and continental Europe. She has been a member of British American Nineteenth Century Historians (BrANCH) since 1995 and has also served as the organization's secretary. She is a fellow of the Royal Historical Society. Emily is now working on enslaved motherhood in an Atlantic context, specifically the roles of enslaved wet-nurses in white antebellum homes. She lives in Reading with her husband and two sons.